Academy of Theatrical Combat

Basics Level I

**Cutlass
Broadsword
Hand to Hand
Quarterstaff**

Includes:
Sample Theatrical Combat
Course Curriculum

by
**Jan Bryant
Dan Speaker
Kim Turney**

Photography by Michael Broussard

Academy of Theatrical Combat Basics Level 1
Copyright © 2012 Academy of Theatrical Combat

All rights reserved. Except for brief passages quoted in newspaper, magazine, radio or television reviews, no part of this book may be reproduced in any form or by any means, electronic or mechanical, including photocopying or recording, or by an information storage and retrieval system, without permission in writing from the publisher.

Professionals and amateurs are hereby warned that this material, being fully protected under the copyright laws of the United States of America and all other countries of the Berne and Universal Copyright Conventions, is subject to a royalty. All rights including, but not limited to, professional, amateur, recording, motion picture, recitation, lecturing, public reading, radio and television broadcasting, and the rights of translation into foreign languages are strictly reserved.

Printed in the United States of America

First Printing, 2012

ISBN 978-0-9885089-0-3

Cover design and layout by Kim Turney

Published by
Academy of Theatrical Combat
13556 Beaver Street
Sylmar, CA 91342

www.theatricalcombat.com

Acknowledgements

We would like to thank Michael 'Mikey' Broussard for being so patient and understanding as he took hundreds and hundreds of photos so we could decide what we needed for this book. We also want to thank our additional photo contributors, Patty Jean Robinson, Garrett Shultz Lynette Privatsky and Eric Hunter, for lighting it all.

A special thanks to James Lew. Along with contributing photos to this book, James has inspired us in our work in so many ways.

We also thank our students, the stars, and the directors we have worked with, who over the years, have motivated us to create and continue to refine our methodology of training.

Introduction

This is a documentation of drills and techniques as they are taught at the Academy of Theatrical Combat's ongoing Basics Level 1 training class. The information contained in this book should be used in conjunction with proper instruction. The curriculum of the Academy has a scaffold structure using basic level skills and techniques to lay the foundation for subsequent skills and techniques. Practicing each drill repeatedly trains the movement into the performer's muscles and allows them to develop their skill as a thinking fighter.

Working on drills with a partner is essential in selling the illusion of violence in performance. Partners must share absolute trust and are responsible for each other's safety. Learning to communicate and preserve each other's trust in a safe environment is a key component of this curriculum.

Assimilating these techniques will give the performer freedom to focus on telling their character's story through fight movement, but there is more to Theatrical Combat than just assimilating the techniques. Theatrical Combat is a form of storytelling. How to PERFORM the fight, including motivation, phrasing and tempo of fights will be discussed in Basics Level 2. The Level 1 techniques should be mastered before performance energy is added.

The goal of the Academy of Theatrical Combat is to give performers all the tools they need to feel confident in any action situation for stage, film, television, motion capture, or internet production. This includes knowing theatrical combat techniques so well, they become second nature and allow the actor to adapt safely and effectively to any and all situations they might face as performers.

Jan Bryant and Hans Pasricha review the Motion Capture shotlist

Kim Turney on the set of Fight Night

Dan watches the monitors on the Motion Capture set

Disclaimer: You are using the information in *Academy of Theatrical Combat Basics Level 1* at your own risk. The Academy of Theatrical Combat is not liable for any injury, mishap or wound of any kind that may occur while you are practicing the skills and techniques in this publication. We recommend that you comply with all the SAFETY NOTES in this publication and that you study under the supervision of an instructor of Theatrical Combat, sometimes referred to as Stage Combat.

Table of Contents

Cutlass — 7

- Cutlass Targets — 14
- Cutlass Parry System — 18
- Cutlass Drills and Techniques — 27
- Cutlass Basic Fight Choreography — 31

Broadsword — 33

- Broadsword Parry System — 36
- Broadsword Drills and Techniques — 45
- Broadsword Basic Fight Choreography — 48

Hand to Hand Techniques — 49

- Slap and Punch Reactions — 50
- Slap — 52
- Crossing Punch — 57

Quarterstaff — 63

- Quarterstaff Parry System — 64
- Quarterstaff Drills — 76
- Quarterstaff Basic Fight Choreography — 80

About the Sword Masters — 82

Sample Theatrical Combat Course Curriculum — 85

Appendix — 97

CUTLASS

The Cutlass is what we think of when we imagine pirate sword fights. The cutlass was derived from a big knife, which was very useful for fighting in the small spaces onboard ships. It lends itself to a basic and brutal style of fighting. Since the cutting action with this weapon is the foundation of some of the simpler styles of fighting and a shorter weapon is easier to control, it is a very good choice for beginning training in the use of any cutting weapon. The cutlass has a very distinct edge so the performer knows intuitively which side of the blade is the cutting edge.

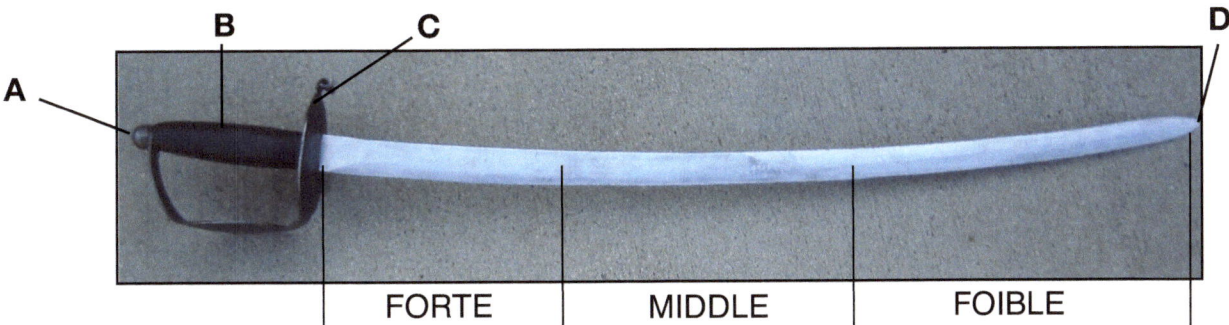

Parts of The Cutlass

A The POMMEL is used to hold the sword together. It is also the counterbalance for the blade so that on a well balanced sword the center of balance is close to the hand making it easier to manipulate. The pommel can also be used for striking when the fighting gets too close to use the blade.

B The HANDLE, or GRIP, is the place to hold the sword.
The TANG is the part of the blade that goes through the handle. The end of the tang is usually threaded to attach the pommel.

C The GUARD comes in many shapes and sizes depending on the weapon and time period, but on all swords it is used to protect the hand while fighting.

The Pommel, Handle and Guard together make up the HILT of the cutlass.

The BLADE has three sections:
The FORTE, or strong part of the blade, is the third of the blade nearest the handle. It is used for parrying or blocking.
The MIDDLE part connects the forte and foible.
The FOIBLE, or weak part of the blade, is the third of the blade nearest the point. It is used for making the attacks on the body since it carries the most power and momentum while making a cut.

The blade has a TRUE EDGE, which we use for making attacks or cuts, just as we do with a knife while chopping vegetables, and a back or FALSE EDGE, which is opposite the true edge. The side of the blade that is wide and flat is called the FLAT of the blade.

D The POINT.

Gripping the Cutlass

The cutlass should be held in a way that makes the best use of its natural balance. If the sword is held too tightly it will be impossible to move with enough dexterity to make the moves look good and the hand will tire out quickly. If the sword is held too loosely or in the weak part of the fingers then the action of the blade becomes wobbly and there is a great risk of losing your sword. The old admonition to hold your sword like you would a bird, '*tightly enough so it won't fly away but loosely enough so you don't choke the life out of it,*' is an excellent image.

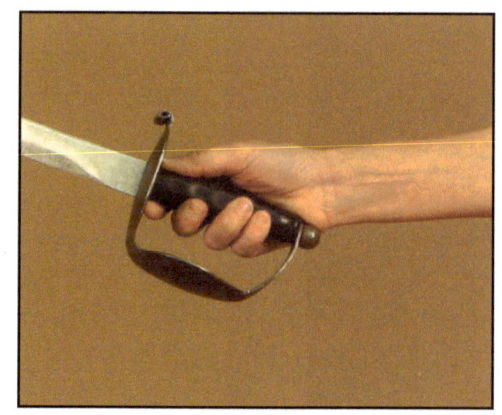

When you hold the cutlass you want to squeeze the handle with the thumb and forefinger opposite each other. The other 3 fingers need to wrap around the handle and hold the handle into the outside muscle of the palm near the heel of the hand. There should be a hollow between the middle of the palm of your hand and the handle of the sword (imagine holding a marble in that hollow). With this grip you should be able to draw circles with the tip of the weapon using your wrist and fingers (and forearm for those really big circles) in a very relaxed fashion as if you were using a paintbrush.

If you are a Video Gamer, gripping the cutlass is almost the identical grip to the way you hold your Game Controller.

On Guard Stance

The ON GUARD stance is designed to give you the best balance and allow you to move smoothly both forwards and backwards with minimal movement in between. If your weight is too far either backwards or forwards you will have to shift your weight onto the other foot before you can move. The same is true for a stance that is too wide. This will produce a visual "hiccup" in movement and make it much more difficult to move quickly.

To find your on guard stance, stand with your feet together at the heels. The toes should be pointing 90 degrees away from each other. The foot pointing forward is on the same side as the hand holding your weapon. This is called FIRST POSITION in fencing or sword fighting.

As you stand in this position with your knees straight try to relax as much as possible. Look in a mirror to see how your shoulders and hips naturally line up about 45 degrees from square forward.

From this position take one step out with both feet (one at a time, of course) so that your heels are under or just outside your hips, and bend your knees keeping the toes pointed in the same directions they were in First Position.

Bring your sword up so that the tip is pointing directly at the center of your chest if you are looking in a mirror. To get the level of the sword positioned correctly imagine there is a laser beam coming out of the tip of the sword. Imagine that beam hitting the center of your chest in the mirror. Keep the palm of the hand holding the sword facing the ground (also called IN PRONATION) so that the true edge of the sword is facing the outside (to the right with the right hand or to the left with the left hand). The forearm of your sword hand should be about parallel to the ground and floating out in front of you with as little tension as possible. The elbow should be approximately a spread hand's width away from your body. The unarmed hand can, for now, can be made into a loose fist and placed on the back hip. The challenge here is to find a relaxed, ready position that is very balanced. Again, your weight should be evenly balanced, or 50/50, between both feet.

Footwork

ADVANCE: Unweight the front of your front foot by lifting the toes inside your shoe. Reach the front heel forward just above the ground and step out as far as you comfortably can. At the same time, push off from the back edge of the back foot and bring it underneath you, returning to your on guard stance. The goal here is to move smoothly (without upward bobbing of the head or any skipping action) and get back on balance as quickly as possible. For example: Imagine you are in a close-up shot on camera. As you advance, you want to make sure your face stays centered in frame.

RETREAT: The reverse of advance, only reach the outside edge of the back foot behind as you push off the heel of the front foot. Then quickly bring the front foot back underneath you. The goal here is to move smoothly (without upward bobbing of the head or any skipping action) and get back on balance as quickly as possible.

PASS FORWARD: Start with the rear foot. Step past the front foot while maintaining the position of the body and the feet (don't shift your hips) then bring the front foot back to the on guard position as quickly as possible. This move will gain much more distance than the Advance or the Retreat.

PASS BACK: The reverse of the Pass Forward starting with the front foot. Be sure to rock off the heel of the front foot as with the Retreat.

LUNGE: Unweight the front of your front foot by lifting the toes inside your shoe. Shoot the front foot forward gliding the heel along the ground as if you were sliding a coin along the floor with your heel. At the same time snap the back leg straight leaving the back foot completely flat on the floor. When the front foot lands, your lower leg should be perpendicular to the floor.

In DEMI LUNGE the upper thigh ends up at an angle to the ground.

In FULL LUNGE the upper thigh ends up parallel to the ground.

Dan demonstrates a DEMI LUNGE while cutting to head.

RECOVER (FROM LUNGE): Flex the back knee as you push off the front heel and snap back to on guard. The body should move directly back with no lift in the torso.

RECOVER FORWARD (FROM LUNGE): Push off the back edge of the back foot, bring the back leg forward to on guard.

REVERSE GUARD: When the leg opposite the weapon side is forward. Moving into Reverse Guard from Regular (or Right) On Guard or into Regular (or Right) On Guard from Reverse Guard is called CHANGING GUARD.

CHANGE GUARD FORWARD: The back foot moves forward to change guard. The alignment of the hips, shoulders and feet change to reflect the new on guard position.

CHANGE GUARD BACK: The front foot moves backward to change guard. The alignment of the hips, shoulders and feet change to reflect the new on guard position.

SLIP LEFT: A move to the left stepping with the left foot first and bringing the right foot back to on guard.

SLIP RIGHT: A move to the right stepping with the right foot first and bringing the left foot back to on guard.

Distance

DISTANCE is the amount of space between you and your fight partner allowing both of you to execute all of your sword moves safely while creating an illusion of violence.

There are 3 distances we refer to while setting up a swordfight.

Dan and Jan demonstrate ON GUARD DISTANCE.

OUT OF DISTANCE: The distance where you are so far away from each other that your weapons cannot come in contact. This is a good place to "stalk" or "size up" an adversary in a piece of choreography. It is also the place to break off an engagement dramatically or for safety reasons.

ON GUARD DISTANCE: The distance where weapons can cross but still far enough away so that you cannot make a believable attack on your partner's body. If you are in a proper on guard stance facing a partner there should be an overlap of blades of about three inches.

Dan and Jan demonstrate ATTACK DISTANCE.

ATTACK DISTANCE: This is the distance from which we do most of our fighting. It is close enough to make a believable attack on the body and yet it is far enough away so that the tip of the blade cannot hit our partner. This is a critical place to practice since it allows you to make believable attacks and yet keeps everyone safe while developing weapon control.

Finding Safe Distance

Finding SAFE DISTANCE.

You can find your safe distance by coming on guard, reaching out your arm so that it is straight with the point directed at the middle of your partner's chest and taking one large advance in (or several small ones) until the point of your cutlass is about 6 inches away from the closest targets. From this distance your partner should be able to parry, or block, an incoming attack with their weapon. As long as neither partner leans in, there should be no way to hit their body.

Cutting With a Cutlass

IMPACT CUT: A direct strike with the cutting edge of the blade to the body. The strike occurs most efficiently at the end point of the swing's arc.

DRAW CUT: Dragging the edge of the blade across the body to slice the flesh.

MAGIC FORCE FIELD
Visualize your partner with a FORCE FIELD 1 to 2 feet out from their body. Chop at that force field with energy and stop the forward chopping action by letting the blade bounce off the magic force field (there should be just enough bounce to stop the sword, not a pulling away from target with energy). This gives the illusion of power being blocked without letting the energy reach your partner's sword or body.

REVERSAL OF TENSION

When cutting with a sword you need to have a "brake" at the end of the cutting action in order to control the force of the swing. This brake is called REVERSAL OF TENSION. Imagine trying to pound in a nail with a hammer. At the point of impact there is a squeezing of the muscles to maximize the accuracy of your swing and stop the hammer. This is a similar action to making impact cuts with a sword. Reversal of Tension will save many blades from breaking and give both the attacker and defender confidence that they can perform safely. To get the feel of using Reversal of Tension when you cut, repeat the following drills several times.

Cutting Drill

Do this drill while facing your partner with their blade down at their side, or while facing yourself in the mirror.

Practice this drill with both the right and left hand.

Advance and Cut to head
Cut to Chest (palm up, or supinated)
Cut to Shoulder (palm down, or pronated)
Retreat

Magic Force Field Drill

Do this drill while facing your partner, or while facing yourself in the mirror.

Practice this drill with both the right and left hand.

A	B
Beat Blade away	Accept Beat, relax the point of the weapon down and to the side
Advance and Cut to Force Field all around partner's body	Get used to having the blade come at you
Retreat to on guard	Return to on guard
Accept Beat, relax the point of the weapon down and to the side	Beat Blade away
Get used to having the blade come at you	Advance and Cut to Force Field all around partner's body
Return to on guard	Retreat to on guard

SAFETY NOTE:
While doing these or any weapons drills, always keep the tip of your weapon from drawing across your partner's face.

Targeting

When making an attack, you target a very specific point on your partner's body. If you are cutting at the belly, you need to look at the specific point on your partner's belly that you are trying to "hit" (such as the belly button) and cut at that specific point, stopping the energy outside of the magic force field.

Looking to target helps make the attack more accurate since the hand will follow where your eyes look. Looking to target also gives the audience and your partner a clue as to what is going to happen next.

Another benefit of looking to target is that it encourages you to continually change your focus. Using a soft or roving focus can help keep you connected with everything that is going on around you, allowing you to stay in the moment.

Communicating With Your Partner

It is very important to keep checking in with your partner visually. Looking back to their face occasionally can help you stay in tune with one another. In certain situations we use an "eye cue" to let our partner know when and where we are going to make an attack.

As you practice, it is also a good idea to help each other verbally stay in touch as well, so go ahead and talk to one another as you go through each drill.

Breathing and Relaxation

It is very important to remember to relax and breathe while you are training. Holding your breath can create tension throughout your body. Breathing will allow you to move easily and maintain your energy and concentration.

A good way to assure that you are breathing during your drills is to verbally call out the names of the parries and/or targets as you go. Talking will encourage you to breath and breathing will help keep your muscles relaxed and supple.

Precision vs. Speed

The first thing most people want to do when they hold a sword is to swing it fast and make a dramatic whooshing sound. This is perfectly acceptable as a warm up before you begin working with a partner. Once you start working with a partner, it is important to focus on being precise with your cuts so that eventually, no matter how fast you are going, you will be able to target the cutting edge of your weapon exactly where you choose.

CUTLASS TARGETS

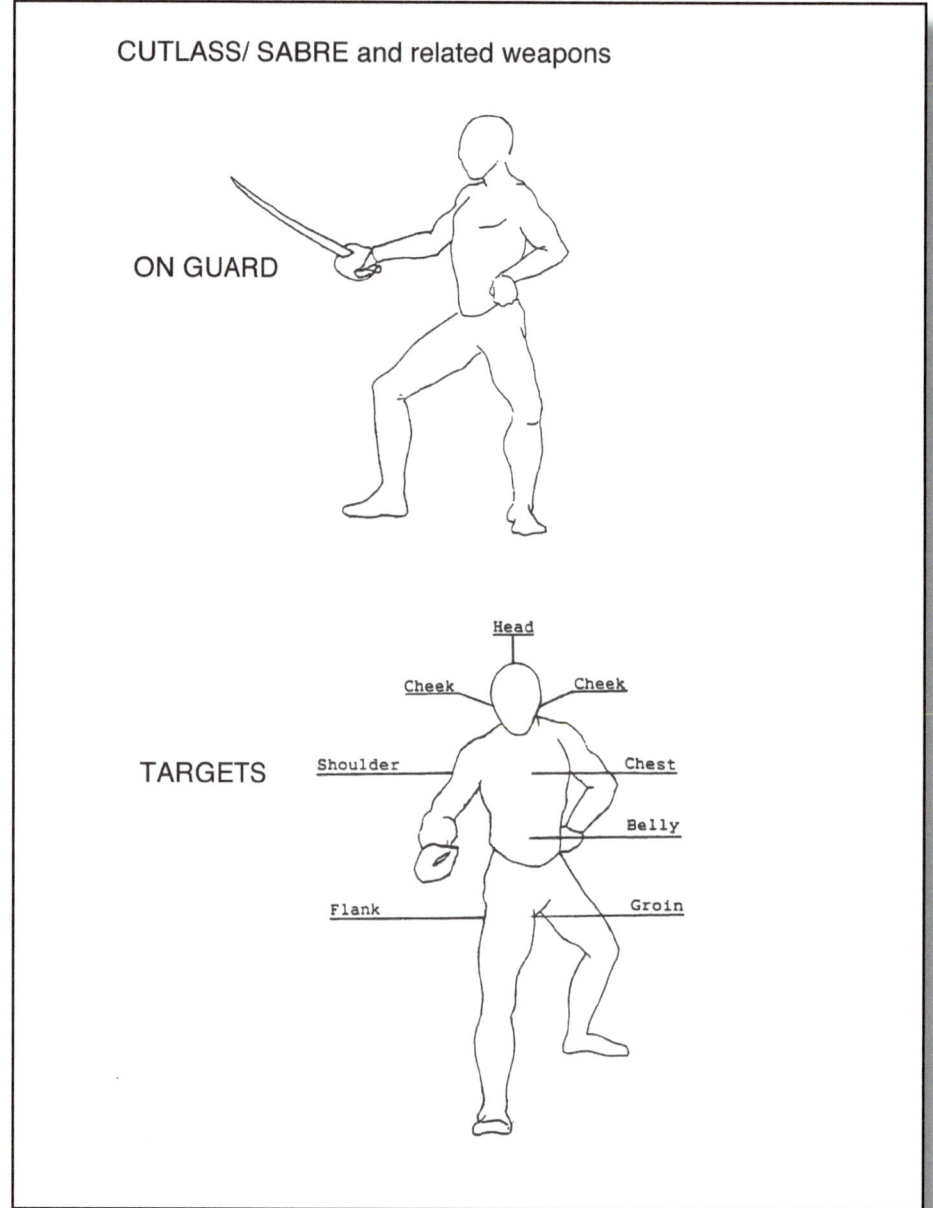

NOTE:
The Cheek targets shown above will be covered thoroughly in *Academy of Theatrical Combat Basics Level 2.*

SAFETY NOTE:

PROTECT THE "MONEY"

In Basics Level 1, the face is never targeted. Our students are actors and we also work with high level stars, and their face means money. If they get injured in any way, it could cost the production a lot of money and everyone involved with the production their job. So Protect the "Money" at All Times!

The Belly Target
is at the belly button level.

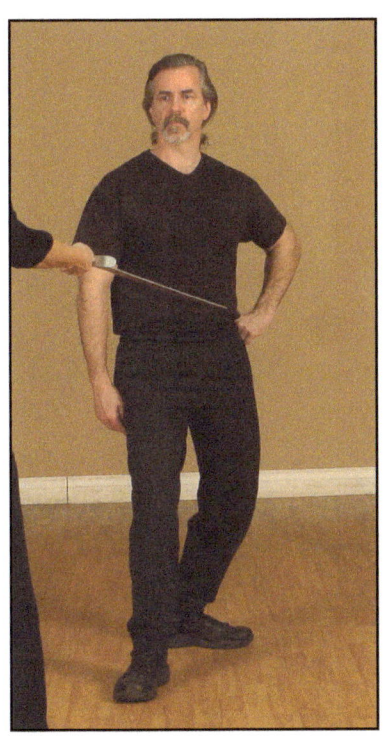

The Flank Target
is the outside of the upper thigh, at the juncture of the thigh and hip joint.

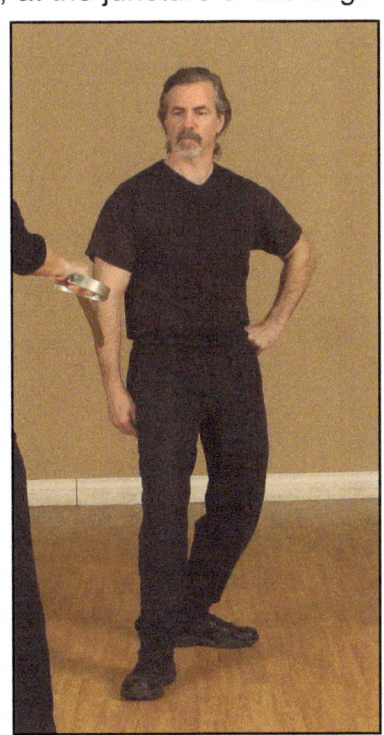

The Shoulder Target
is where the deltoid muscle meets the bicep muscle in the upper arm.

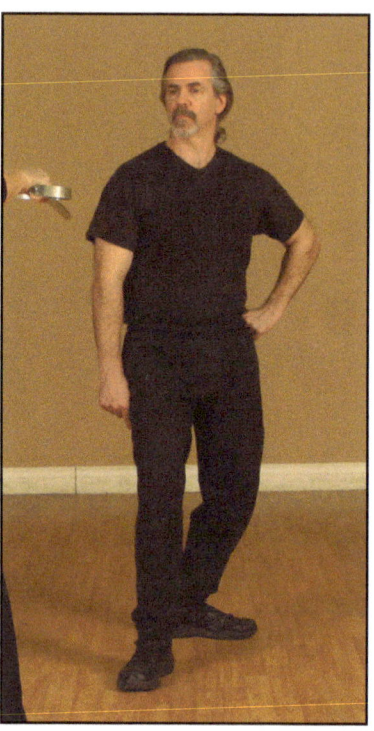

The Chest Target
is the center of your chest.

The Head Target
is actually the top of the forehead, not the top of the head. This target is the same for both parries 5 & 9.

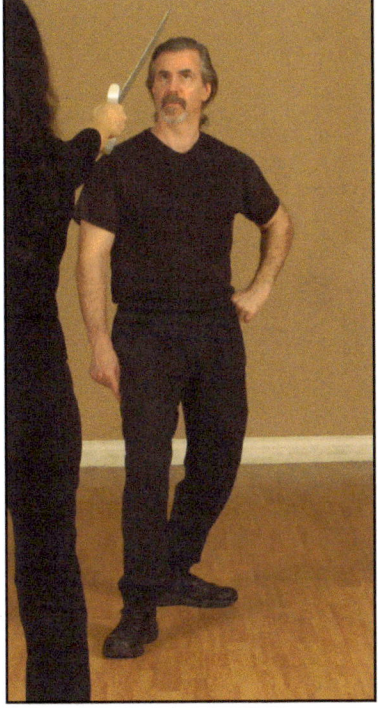

The Groin Target
is the upper inner thigh where the femoral artery is located. Slicing this artery open would put your opponent out of commission almost instantly.

CUTLASS PARRY SYSTEM

NOTES:
All parries are out in front of your body (including the front knee) as if you were creating an imaginary shield, or MAGIC FORCE FIELD. All parries are made with the elbow bent.

The move into each parry should deflect attacks outward, away from the body.

The Parry System for all weapons used at the Academy is derived from the French Classical Parry System.

PARRY 1 is made with the point down, crossguard just below the chest, as if looking at a watch on the wrist of the weapon hand. **Parry 1 protects the Belly.**

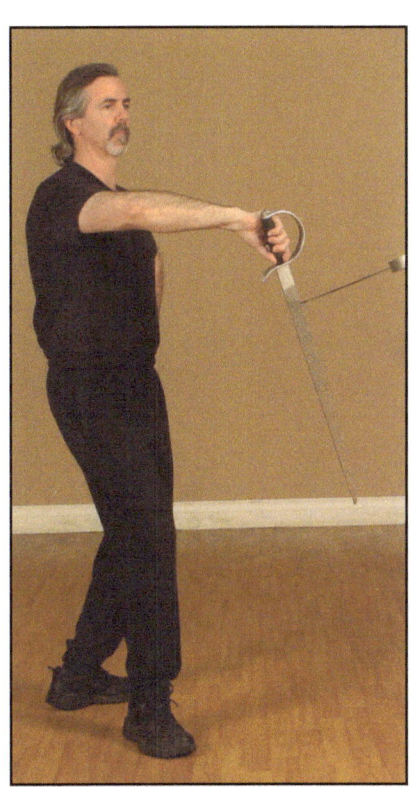

PARRY 2 is low and to the outside, point down with the blade angled slightly to match the angle of the upper thigh on the front leg. The wrist should be straight and the shoulders relaxed. **Parry 2 protects the Flank.**

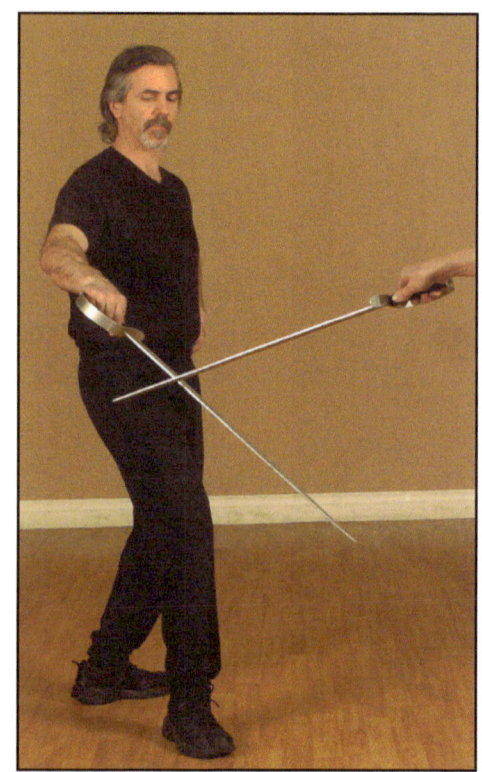

PARRY 3 is made with the point up, the hand a little higher than the waist and pushed out slightly away from the body. **Parry 3 protects the Shoulder.**

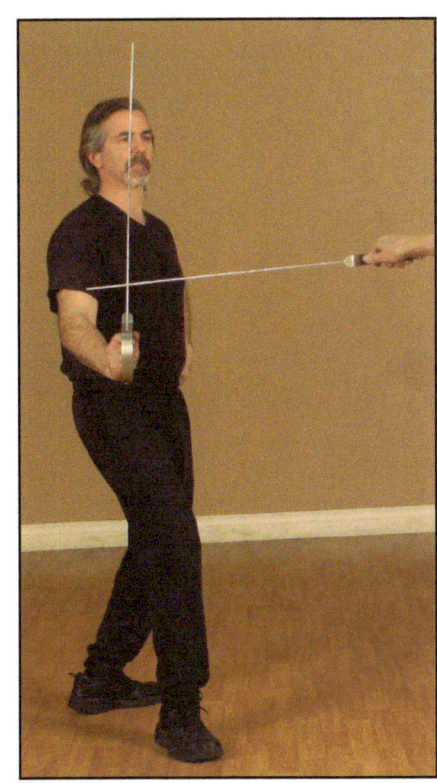

PARRY 4 has the point straight up and the hand a little higher than the waist. **Parry 4 protects the Chest.**

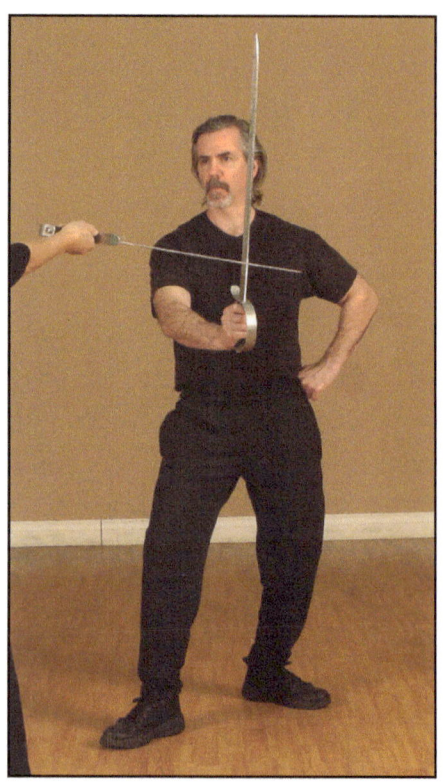 

PARRY 5 is held square over the head, out in front of your front knee with the hand to the outside of your body. **Parry 5 protects the Head.**

PARRY 7 protects the Groin area, specifically the femoral artery in the upper inner thigh. The palm of the hand faces up, in supination, and the blade angles down.

PARRY 9, also known as the "alternate head parry," is held square above the head, out in front of the front knee, with the hand to the inside of the body. **Parry 9 protects the Head.**

PARRY 6 protects the Shoulder, utilizing the back edge of the blade. The palm of the hand faces up, in supination, and the blade angles up. Parry 6 is not normally used with a cutlass since it is not a very effective parry for a cutting weapon.

Parry 6 is not included in the Basic Cutlass Drills.

PARRY 8 utilizes the back edge of the blade. The palm of the hand faces up, in supination, and the blade angles down. **Parry 8 protects the Flank.** Parry 8 is not normally used with a cutlass since it is not a very effective parry for a cutting weapon.

Parry 8 is not included in the Basic Cutlass Drills.

Cutlass Drills and Techniques

Basic Cutlass Techniques

BEAT ATTACK: From on guard distance, **A** beats **B's** sword out of the way using the back edge of the blade before advancing into attack distance.

DROP AND ROLL: After your partner beats your blade out of the way, you can transition to Parry 1 by executing what we call a "drop and roll" move. Drop and roll simply means to drop the tip of your weapon towards the ground and roll the blade across in front of you ("drawing" a line with the point of your blade between you and your partner) to the proper Parry 1 position. Executing this move from on guard means the sword stays safely pointed towards the ground and away from your partner's face. We also use this move to get to Parry 5 from the on guard position.

SUPPLE AND ROLL: With the hand in supination (palm up), supple, or flex, the wrist to draw the point across to the other side of the body. This move is used to keep the sword pointed safely away from your partner's body when moving from Parry 7 to Parry 9.

TOUR D'EPEE: After you beat your partner's blade out of the way, you will continue circling the blade into position for your next attack. This circular move of the blade (with the point up) in front of your body is called a Tour d'Epee.

Basic Cutlass Drills

A attacks in all lines while advancing, **B** parries each attack while retreating, then repeat with **B** attacking **A**. The first attack includes closing the distance from On GUARD to IN DISTANCE. These drills should be practiced with the right and left hand.

Basic Cutlass Drill 1 or "1,2,3,4,5,7,9"

A	B
Beat, Tour d'epee	Accept the beat, drop and roll to
Advance Cut Belly	Small Retreat Parry 1
Advance Cut Flank	Retreat Parry 2
Advance Cut Shoulder	Retreat Parry 3
Advance Cut Chest	Retreat Parry 4
Advance Cut Head	Retreat Parry 5
Advance Cut Groin	Retreat Parry 7
Advance Cut Head	Retreat, supple and roll to Parry 9
Retreat to on guard, moving your point away from your partner's hilt and face.	When your partner's blade has cleared yours and your partner has retreated out of distance, return to on guard.

Basic Cutlass Drill 2 or "5,4,3,2,1,7,9"

A	B
Beat, Tour d'Epee	Accept the beat, drop, roll and lift to
Advance Cut Head	Small Retreat Parry 5
Advance Cut Chest	Retreat Parry 4
Advance Cut Shoulder	Retreat Parry 3
Advance Cut Flank	Retreat Parry 2
Advance Cut Belly	Retreat Parry 1
Advance Cut Groin	Retreat Circle Blade Parry 7
Advance Cut Head	Retreat, supple and roll to Parry 9
Retreat to on guard, moving your point away from your partner's hilt and face.	When your partner's blade has cleared yours and your partner has retreated out of distance, return to on guard.

SWIPES: Cue the swipe by making eye contact with your partner and lifting your weapon in prep for the swing. Drop your eyes to the swipe target (belly, foot, etc.) and watch for your partner to begin their evasion (jumping back, ducking, etc.). As soon as your partner is out of the way, swipe the weapon through the space where they were as quickly as possible to create the illusion that you are trying to slash your partner open. Make sure you look to where your partner *was* before the evasion as you swipe your sword through the empty space!

SAFETY NOTE:
SWIPES
Do not begin the swipe until your partner clears
the space you are targeting.
If they don't move, you don't swing.

BIND: Taking control of your partner's blade, transporting it from any line in a half circle to the opposite diagonal line. Frequently we "cast off" the blade at the end of a bind to go on to the next move.

Bind Swipe Drill

A	B
Lunge and Cut to Flank	Parry 2
Ride Bind, Prep for Evasion	Bind, Cast Off Blade
Evade Back	(Cue: 1. Lift Blade Point Up/ Make Eye Contact, 2. Look to Belly) Swipe Belly
	Rectify distance with partner using advance or pass forward.
Parry 2	Lunge and Cut to Flank
Bind, Cast Off Blade	Ride Bind, Prep for Evasion
(Cue: 1. Lift Blade Point Up/ Make Eye Contact, 2. Look to Belly) Swipe Belly	Evade Back

Footwork drills for Fight Class.

CORPS-A-CORPS: Or body to body, happens when fighters close distance to make a grab for their opponent, hit them with a fist, or shove them off balance. The weapons are ineffective at this distance because the fighters are too close to swing with power. Often the weapons are pushed off to the side as the combatants come into physical contact.

Front
CORPS-A-CORPS

Side
CORPS-A-CORPS

PUSH: The push is a partnered action that has 2 beats. The first beat starts with body contact and a flexing of the knees, also called a chug. On the second beat the person being pushed controls their own action to move away from the pusher, who follows that energy creating the illusion of a real push.

EVASIONS: The most common basic evasions are the Duck, the Jump Back, the Jump Up, Slipping Sideways, Twisting out of the way and Running Away.

CUTLASS BASIC FIGHT CHOREOGRAPHY

A	B
Beat, Tour d'Epee	Accept Beat, drop roll lift to
Advance Cut Head	Retreat Parry 5
Advance Cut Chest	Retreat Parry 4
Lunge and Cut Flank	Retreat Parry 2
Accept Bind, recover back leg slightly forward	Bind to 4 (casting their blade away)
Jump Back to evade Belly Swipe	(Cue: 1. Lift Blade Point Up/ Make Eye Contact, 2. Look to Belly) Swipe Belly
	Pass Forward, Tour d'Epee to
Parry 3	Cut Shoulder
Retreat Parry 7	Advance Cut Groin
Retreat Parry (full circle to) 2	Advance Cut Flank
Retreat Parry 1	Lunge and Cut Belly
Bind	Accept Bind
Change Guard Forward to Side Corps-a-corps	Recover Forward for balance
Push	'Stumble' Back from push
(Cue: 1. Lift Blade Point Up/ Make Eye Contact, 2. Look to Belly) Swipe Belly	Jump Back to evade Belly Swipe
Cut Belly	Parry 1
Retreat Parry 4	Advance Cut Chest
Advance Cut Flank	Retreat Parry 2
Retreat Parry 3	Advance Cut Shoulder
Lunge Cut Head	Retreat Parry 5
Accept Bind, try to re-attack	Bind to 7 (casting their blade away)
React to Killing Blow and Die	Kill (Impact cut to ribs, Draw cut away)

To see performance videos of the Cutlass Basic Fight, visit us on
Youtube.com/AcademyFightClass

BROADSWORD

BROADSWORD is a term that has been used to describe many different weapons throughout history. It has been applied to everything from medieval knights' swords to military basket-hilts; from two-handed great swords to Chinese kung-fu swords. This is because the blades of these swords are wider than other common styles of sword blades.

The Academy uses a HAND AND A HALF, or BASTARD, sword for training purposes. This was a very popular weapon used for many centuries in European warfare. It was often used one handed, but could be aided with the other hand at the pommel.

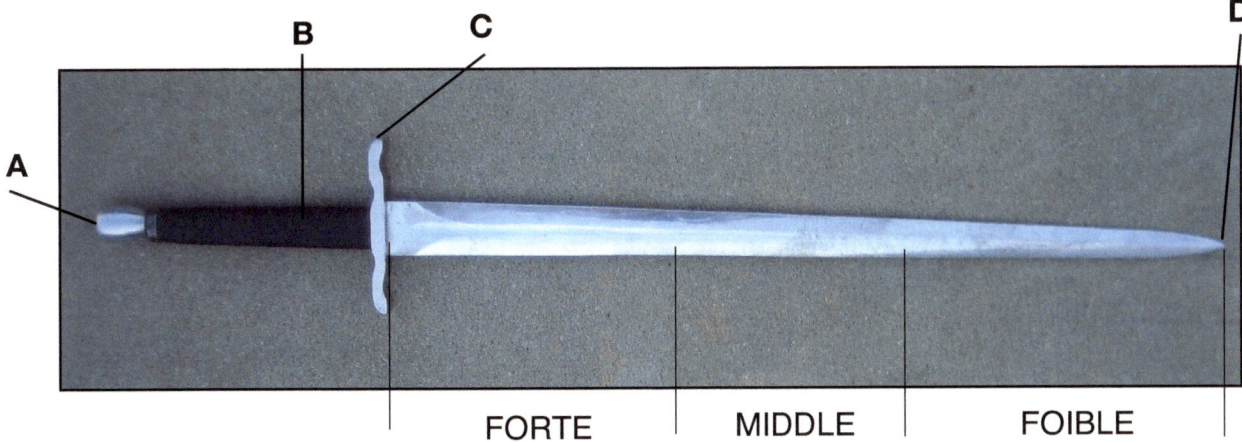

Parts of the Broadsword

A The POMMEL is used to hold the sword together. It is also the counter balance for the blade so that on a well-balanced sword the center of balance is close to the hand, making it easier to manipulate. The pommel can also be used for striking when the fighting gets too close to use the blade.

B The HANDLE, or GRIP, is the place to hold the sword.
The TANG is the part of the blade that goes through the handle. The end of the tang is usually threaded to attach the pommel.

C The GUARD, also called the CROSS GUARD, comes in many shapes and sizes depending on the weapon and time period. On all swords it is used to protect the hand while fighting.

The Pommel, Handle and Guard together make up the HILT of the broadsword.

The BLADE has three sections, the FORTE, the MIDDLE and the FOIBLE just as it does with the cutlass.

The blade has a TRUE EDGE, which we use for making attacks or cuts. The FALSE EDGE, which is also a sharp edge on a broadsword, is opposite the true edge. The side of the blade that is wide and flat is called the FLAT of the blade.

D The POINT.

Gripping the Broadsword

When you hold the broadsword you want to find a way to balance the weight between the fingers and the palm of the controlling hand. With European broadsword the controlling hand is the one in front or closest to the guard. For the purposes of training we will concentrate on using the right hand. Left-handed people of the day were retrained at a very young age because left-handedness was considered "evil." It is a good idea to train on both sides (both right and left) for the purpose of creating balanced muscles so even though our drills will be primarily on the right we encourage you to try them on the left as well.

Start by gripping the sword in your right hand only. Hold it in an open "hand shake" manner with the forefinger and thumb opposite each other. The webbing of the thumb is opposite the true edge. The other 3 fingers need to wrap around and hold the handle into the outside muscle of the palm near the heel of the hand. Imagine you are holding a big knife and chopping vegetables. This will give you a sense of how the sword should work if you are gripping it correctly.

Take your left hand and place the pommel into the middle of the palm, just inside the webbing of the thumb. If you are gripping the sword correctly you should feel the broadsword balanced evenly in both hands.

Broadsword On Guard Stance

The ON GUARD stance for the broadsword is relaxed and informal. The knees are bent and the weapon side leg is forward. The feet are aligned in the same relationship as with the cutlass on guard, with your front foot pointed towards your partner. Allow the back heel to lift and pivot so the hips and shoulders can be free to square up forward.

Footwork

ADVANCES and RETREATS can be made in the same way you do with a cutlass, with the modification of the back foot position described above in the on guard stance.

DEMI LUNGE: Unweight the front of your front foot by lifting the toes inside your shoe. Shoot the front foot forward gliding the heel along the ground (as if you were sliding a coin along the floor with your heel). At the same time snap the back leg straight leaving the back foot completely flat on the floor. When the front foot lands, your lower leg should be perpendicular to the floor.

DEMI LUNGE RECOVERY: Flex the back knee as you push off the front heel and snap back to on guard. The body should move directly back with no lift in the torso.

PASS FORWARD: Start with the rear foot. Step past the front foot while maintaining the position of the body and the feet (don't shift your hips) and bring the front foot back to the on guard position as quickly as possible. This move will gain much more distance than the Advance or the Retreat.

PASS BACK: The reverse of the Pass Forward starting with the front foot. Be sure to rock off the heel of the front foot as with the retreat.

REVERSE GUARD: When the leg opposite the weapon side is forward. Moving into Reverse Guard from Regular (or Right) On Guard or into Regular (or Right) On Guard from Reverse Guard is called **CHANGING GUARD**.

CHANGE GUARD FORWARD: The back foot moves forward to change guard. The alignment of the hips, shoulders and feet change to reflect the new on guard position.

CHANGE GUARD BACK: The front foot moves backward to change guard. The alignment of the hips, shoulders and feet change to reflect the new on guard position.

CHANGE GUARD INTO LUNGE: At this point in the training we start combining footwork moves. To combine changing guard and a lunge you change guard forward, snapping the back leg straight as you land (heel first) on the new front foot.

Cutting with the Broadsword

The action of cutting with the broadsword is supported by your core muscles and made more powerful by the relaxed spiraling of the body while you swing the blade.

WRINGING CONTRACTION: By wringing your hands together like you are wringing out a towel as you stop the blade at the end of a cut, you create reversal of tension in your arms. This reversal of tension creates the illusion of a powerful and deadly cut, while giving you the control to stop the blade exactly when and where you want. The wringing contraction is particularly important for the **IMPACT CUT** with a broadsword.

IMPACT CUT: A direct strike with the cutting edge of the blade to the body. The strike occurs most efficiently at the end point of the swing's arc.

DRAW CUT: Dragging the edge of the blade across the body to slice the flesh.

BROADSWORD PARRY SYSTEM

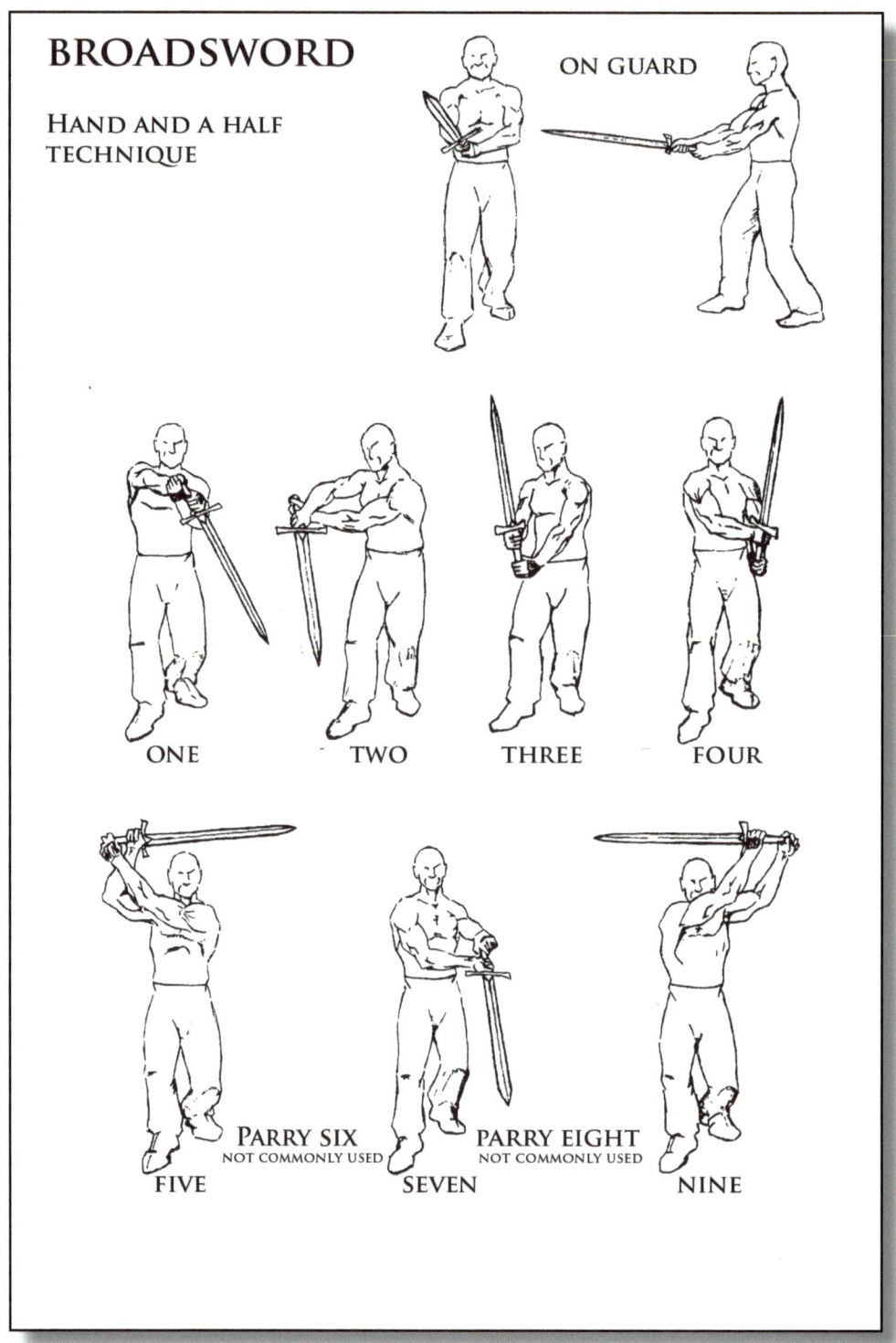

NOTES: All parries are out in front of your body (including the front knee) as if you were creating an imaginary shield, or MAGIC FORCE FIELD, with your weapon positions, .

All parries are made with the elbows bent.

PARRY 1 is made with the point down, crossguard just below the chest as if looking at a watch on the weapon hand. **Parry 1 protects the Belly.**

PARRY 2 is low and to the outside with the point down and slightly in. The wrist should be straight and the shoulders relaxed. **Parry 2 protects the Flank.**

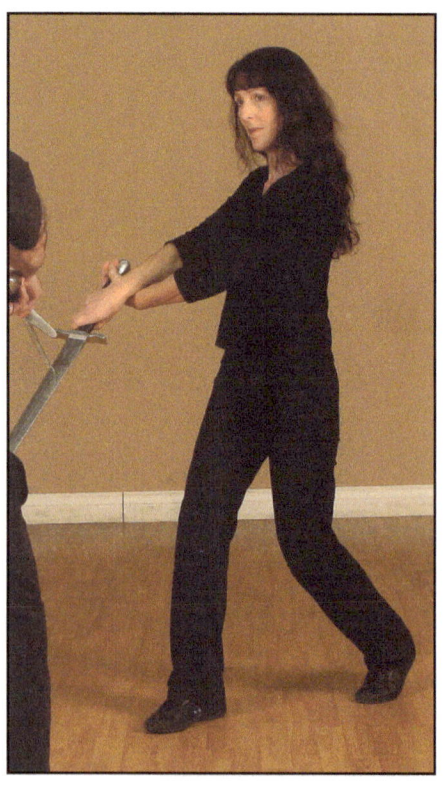

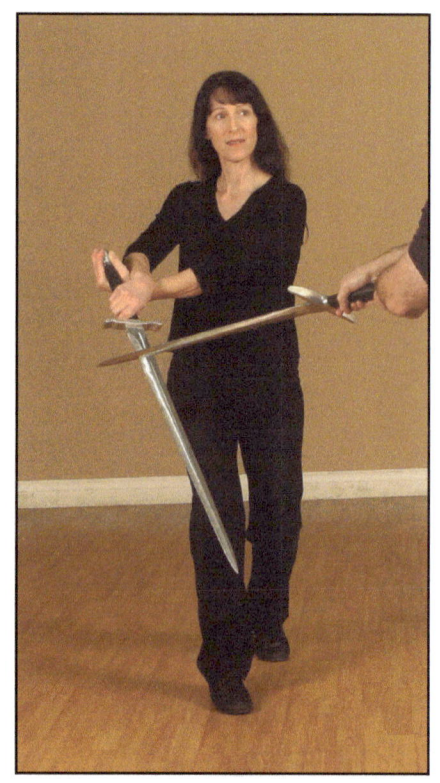

PARRY 3 is made with the point up, the hand a little higher than the waist and pushed out slightly away from the body. **Parry 3 protects the Shoulder.**

PARRY 4 has the point straight up and the hand a little higher than the waist.
Parry 4 protects the Chest.

PARRY 5 is made square above the head, wrists crossed, with the hands to the right.
Parry 5 protects the Head.

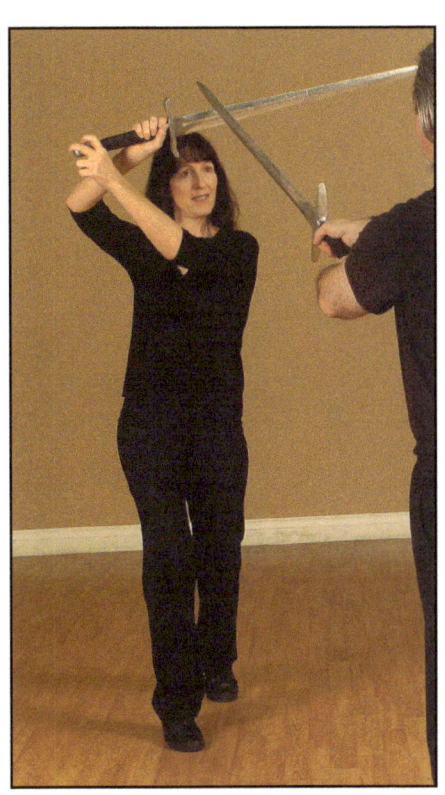

PARRY 7 protects the Groin area, specifically the femoral artery in the upper inner thigh. The palm of the right hand faces up, in supination, and the blade angles down.

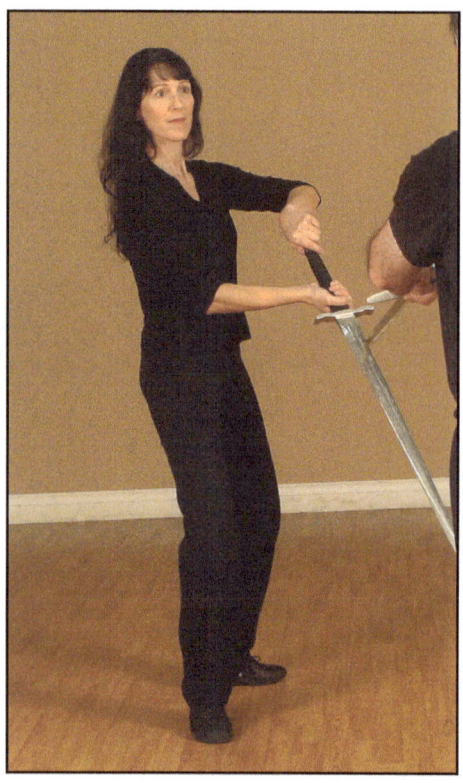

PARRY 9, also known as the "alternate head parry," requires the sword to be held square above the head, wrists uncrossed, with the hands to the left. **Parry 9 protects the Head.**

> **SAFETY NOTE:**
> ***Dropping Your Sword!***
>
> If you drop your sword, do not try to catch it before it hits the ground. Swords can and will bounce. Wait until the sword has stopped moving, then pick it up.

PARRY 6 protects the Shoulder, utilizing the back edge of the blade. The palm of the right hand faces up, in supination, and the blade angles up. Not commonly used with the Broadsword.

Parry 6 is not included in the Basic Broadsword Drills.

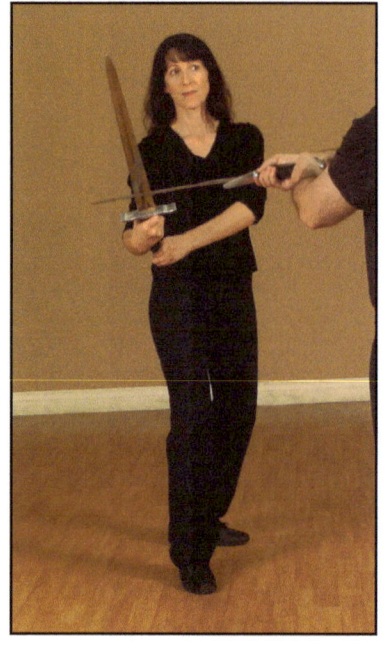

PARRY 8 utilizes the back edge of the blade. The palm of the right hand faces up, in supination, and the blade angles down. **Parry 8 protects the Flank.** Not commonly used with the broadsword.

Parry 8 is not included in the Basic Broadsword Drills.

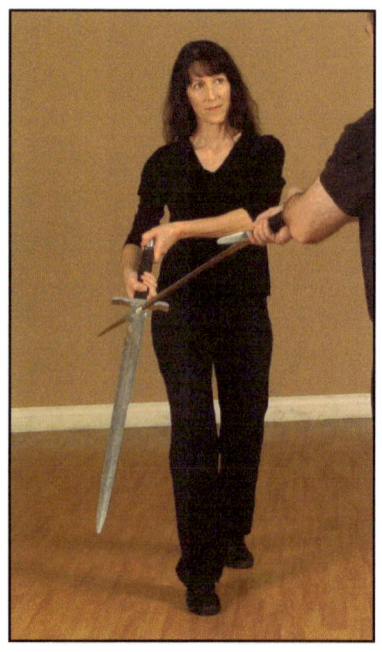

BROADSWORD DRILLS AND TECHNIQUES

Basic Broadsword Techniques

BEAT ATTACK: From on guard distance, **A** beats **B's** sword out of the way using the back edge of the blade before advancing into attack distance.

DROP AND ROLL: After your partner beats your blade out of the way, you can transition to Parry 1 by executing what we call a "drop and roll" move. Drop and roll simply means to drop the tip of your weapon towards the ground and roll the blade across in front of you ("drawing" a line with the point of your blade between you and your partner) to the proper Parry 1 position. Executing this move from on guard means the sword stays safely pointed towards the ground and away from your partner's face. We also use this move to get to Parry 5 from the on guard position.

SUPPLE AND ROLL: With the right hand in supination (palm up), supple, or flex, the wrist to draw the point across to the other side of the body. The left hand is used, levering the sword to control the point here as well. This move is used to keep the sword pointed safely away from your partner's body when moving from Parry 7 to Parry 9.

TOUR D'EPEE: After you beat your partner's blade out of the way, you will continue circling the blade into position for your next attack. This circular move of the blade (with the point up) in front of your body is called a Tour d'Epee.

Cutting Drill

Do this drill while facing your partner with their blade down at their side, or while facing yourself in the mirror.

Advance and Cut to head
Cut to Chest (palm up, or supinated)
Cut to Shoulder (palm down, or pronated)
Retreat

Magic Force Field Drill

Do this drill while facing your partner, or while facing yourself in the mirror.

A	B
Beat, Tour d'Epee	Accept Beat, relax the point of the weapon down and to the side
Advance and Cut to Force Field all around partner's body	Get used to having the blade come at you
Retreat to on guard	Return to on guard
Accept Beat, relax the point of the weapon down and to the side	Beat, Tour d'Epee
Get used to having the blade come at you	Advance and Cut to Force Field all around partner's body
Return to on guard	Retreat to on guard

Bind Swipe Drill

A	B
Lunge and Cut to Flank	Parry 2
Ride Bind, Prep for Evasion	Bind, Cast Off Blade
Evade Back	(cue: 1. Lift Blade Point Up/ Make Eye Contact, 2. Look to Belly) Swipe Belly
	Rectify distance with partner using advance or pass forward.
Parry 2	Lunge and Cut to Flank
Bind, Cast Off Blade	Ride Bind, Prep for Evasion
(cue: 1. Lift Blade Point Up/ Make Eye Contact, 2. Look to Belly) Swipe Belly	Evade Back

Basic Broadsword Drills

A attacks in all lines while advancing, **B** parries each attack while retreating, then repeat with B attacking.

Basic Drill 1 or "1,2,3,4,5,7,9"

A	B
Beat, Tour d'Epee	Accept the beat, drop and roll
Advance Cut Belly	Small Retreat Parry 1
Advance Cut Flank	Retreat Parry 2
Advance Cut Shoulder	Retreat Parry 3
Advance Cut Chest	Retreat Parry 4
Advance Cut Head	Retreat Parry 5
Advance Cut Groin	Retreat Parry 7
Advance Cut Head	Retreat, supple, roll, and lift to Parry 9
Retreat, moving your point away from your partner's hilt and face, back to On Guard.	When your partner's blade has cleared yours and your partner has retreated out of distance, return to on guard.

MIXED FOOTWORK: Using Changes of Guard as well as Advances and Retreats during the drill.

Basic Drill 2 or "5,4,3,2,1,7,9" with Mixed Footwork

A	B
Beat, Tour d'Epee	Accept the beat, drop, roll and lift
Change Guard Forward Cut Head	Change Guard Back Parry 5
Change Guard Forward Cut Chest	Change Guard Back Parry 4
Change Guard Forward Cut Shoulder	Change Guard Back Parry 3
Advance Cut Flank	Retreat Parry 2
Change Guard Forward Cut Belly	Change Guard Back Parry 1
Advance Cut Groin	Retreat Circle Blade Parry 7
Change Guard Forward Cut Head	Change Guard Back, supple, roll, and lift to Parry 9
Change Guard Back, moving your point away from your partner's hilt and face, back to On Guard.	When partner's blade has cleared yours, and your partner has retreated out of distance, return to On Guard.

BROADSWORD BASIC FIGHT CHOREOGRAPHY

A	B
On Guard in Reverse Guard with sword angled down and back to the right	Right On Guard with blade pointing at A
Beat B's blade away, Tour d'Epee	Accept Beat, drop roll lift to
Change Guard Forward and Cut Head	Change Guard Back and Parry 5
Change Guard Forward and Cut Chest	Change Guard Back and Parry 4
Change Guard with a Lunge and Cut Flank	Change Guard Back and Parry 2
Accept Bind	Bind to 4 (cast the blade away)
Jump Back	(Cue: 1. Lift Blade Point Up/ Make Eye Contact, 2. Look to Belly) Swipe Belly
Step back into Reverse Guard and Parry 3	Pass forward Cut Shoulder
Change Guard Back and Parry 7	Change Guard Forward and Cut Groin
Change Guard Back and Parry 2	Change Guard Forward and Cut Flank
Change Guard Back and Parry 1	Change Guard to Lunge and Cut Belly
Bind and Change Guard Forward to Side Corps-a-Corps	Accept Bind
Push	Stumble back
(Cue: 1. Lift Blade Point Up/ Make Eye Contact, 2. Look to Belly) Swipe Belly	Jump Back, releasing the left hand to clear the weapon
Change Guard Forward to Right On Guard (or run forward) and Cut Belly	(Re-grip w/ left hand) Retreat Parry 1
Retreat and Parry 4	Advance and Cut Chest
Change Guard Forward and Cut Flank	Change Guard Back and Parry 2
Retreat and Parry 3	Advance and Cut Shoulder
Change guard to Lunge and Cut Head	Change Guard Back and Parry 5
	Bind to 7 (cast the blade away)
React to Killing Blow and Die	Kill (Impact cut to ribs, draw cut away)

To see performance videos of the Broadsword Basic Fight, visit us on

Youtube.com/AcademyFightClass

HAND TO HAND TECHNIQUES
Basic Movement for Hand to Hand

Twisting or pivoting on your feet while staying centered is a vital part of most everything we do in hand to hand. Start by standing with your feet apart facing forward. Twist from side to side, keeping the weight 50/50 on both feet allowing the back heel to come off the floor. Allow the arms to swing freely with the upper body relaxed and upright. This motion is the basis for reactions for hits to the face, and for the look of power behind a strike.

The Twisting Drill

SLAP AND PUNCH REACTIONS

Slap Reaction

Imagine a blow to the face. Place your own hand on your cheek and push with a short sharp energy allowing your head to snap sideways with your neck relaxed. This should give you a sense of how your head would react to a slap. Make sure you warm up your neck before doing this so you don't make yourself sore or pull a muscle!

SAFETY NOTE:
Contact is made to the face with your hand for drill purposes only. Do not make contact with the face when actually performing a slap.

Punch Reaction

Now use this energy to imagine a harder blow, like a punch, and allow the shoulders and hips to follow the energy of the head, twisting on your feet as with the basic twisting drill. Reactions need to reflect the amount of energy in the blow, so a slap reaction will have less movement than a punch reaction or a kick to the face reaction.

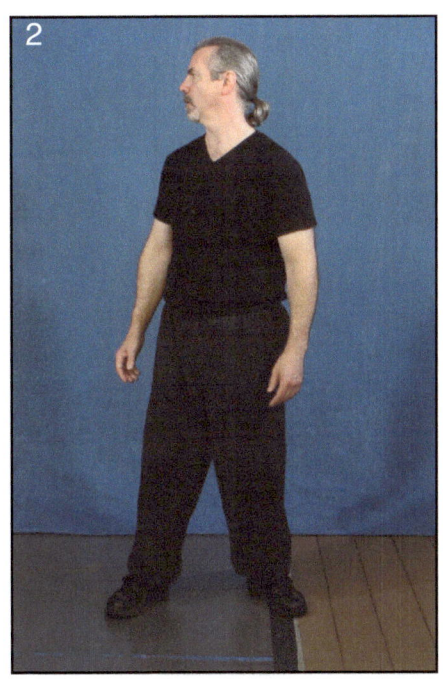

SLAP

A SLAP is a strike with the relaxed open palm of the hand usually delivered to the face. It can also be delivered with the back of an open hand. This is called a BACKHAND.

> ### SAFETY NOTE:
> ### SLAPS!
> The Slap is one of the most dangerous moves in theatrical combat for the simple reason that NO ONE THINKS A SLAP IS DANGEROUS.

The truth is, the force of a slap can dislocate a jaw or detach the retina of the eye. If the slap makes contact with the neck it can rupture lymph nodes. If the slap makes contact with an ear, it can rupture the eardrum. If fingernails rake an eye it could cause permanent damage. This list of possible injuries goes on. Being able to handle the pain of a slap once or twice is not the same as having to do it over and over again in a performance situation where performance adrenaline often makes these blows unpredictable. Rest assured that if you are taking a slap for film, there will never just be one or two takes. If you are doing stage, this action has to be performed in rehearsal as well as the number of performances the production requires! It is very important to practice a blow to the face so it looks real without having to make contact.

To counter the danger of the slap, SAFETY FACTORS must be observed from the very beginning of learning this technique.

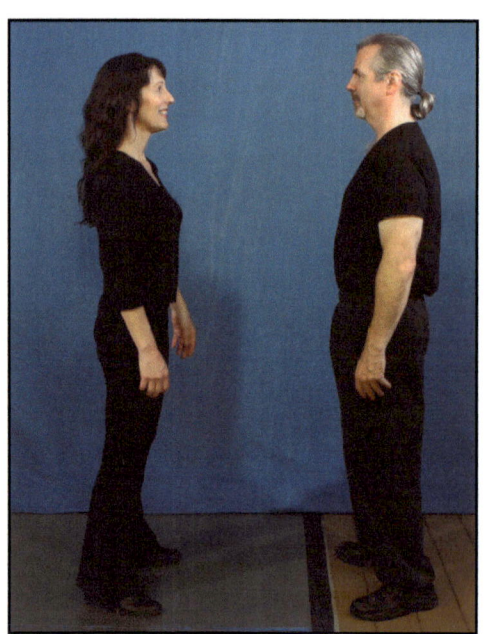

FINDING SAFE DISTANCE: In order to find a safe distance for the slap, start by SQUARING UP with your partner. To square up, stand facing your partner with your centers lined up, both of you should have your feet apart with your weight balanced evenly. (Left)

The person delivering the slap reaches out placing his/her fingertips on the front of their partner's shoulders standing at arms length. This is called MEASURING SAFE DISTANCE. (Right)

GETTING INTO FIGHT STANCE: The attacker takes a step back with the slapping side. This is the basic **FIGHT STANCE**.

TESTING THE DISTANCE: You can test the safe distance by extending the slapping hand and moving it across the target. As long as neither partner leans forward, there is no way for the slap to actually make contact and you can use real energy when moving through that empty space.

The Three Part Cue

Start in fight stance with both arms relaxed to the sides, ready to do the Three Part Cue – reach out towards your the partner's shoulder with the front hand, TOUCH CUE, making eye contact, EYE CUE, with your partner and raising the slapping hand, VISUAL CUE. These three cues happen simultaneously as the First Beat of the Slap Technique.

For the VISUAL CUE, the slapping hand is raised to the side with an open relaxed palm as if you were waving to someone.

NOTE: Keep your slapping hand in your peripheral vision in line with your shoulder.

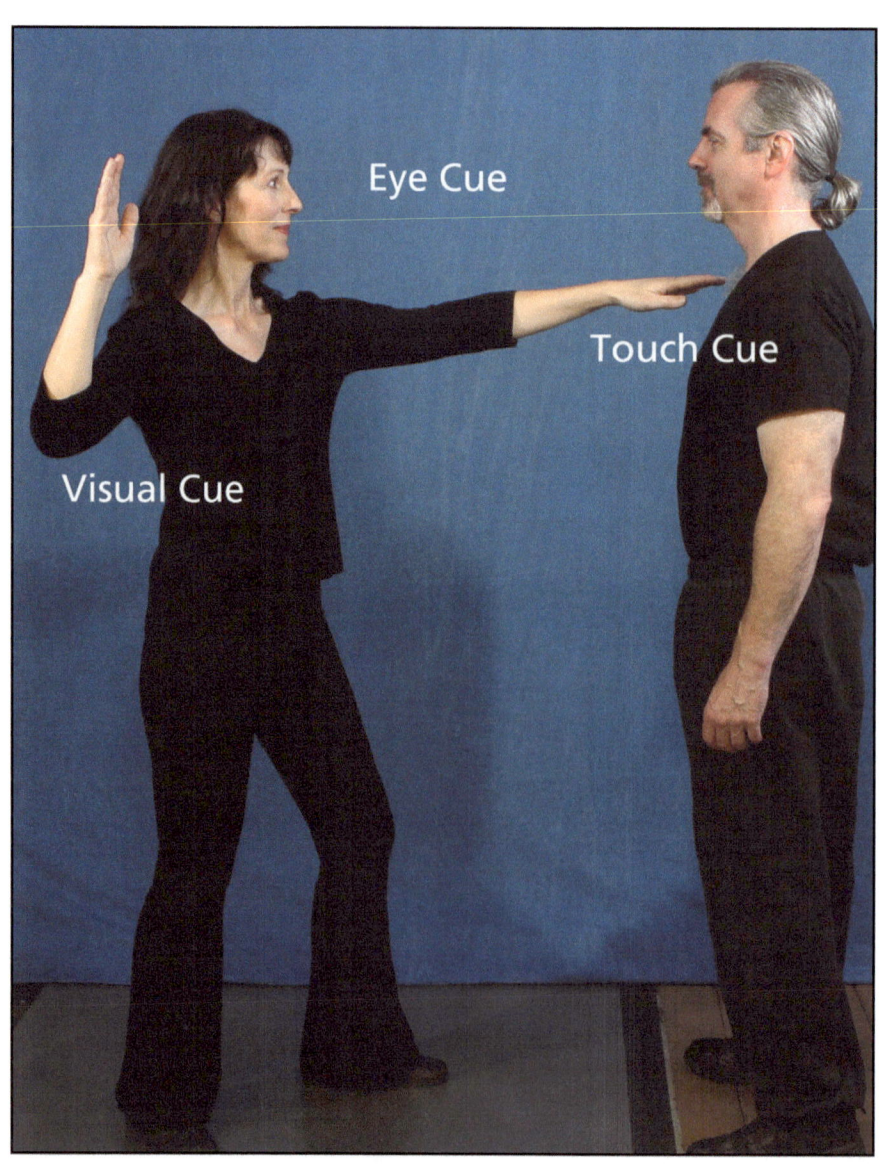

On the Second Beat of the Slap Technique, the slapping hand passes in front of the face at cheekbone level, the **TOUCH CUE** arm counters the move by recoiling in, and the recipient snaps the head in reaction as the hand passes the point of imaginary impact. The attacker follows through by twisting the body in the direction of the slap and allowing the arm to drop naturally. You can practice the relaxed feel of a slap by slapping your other hand out in front of you brushing past it in an arc. Notice how the hand reacts to the impact so you can simulate this reaction while slapping the air.

3 Part Cue for Slap

Safety Note: The fingers point upwards on the slapping hand for safety as the slapping hand passes in front of the face...

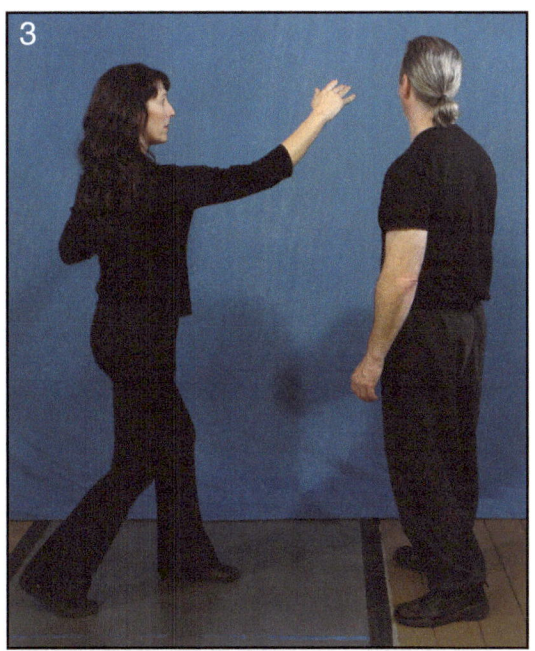

...At cheekbone level.

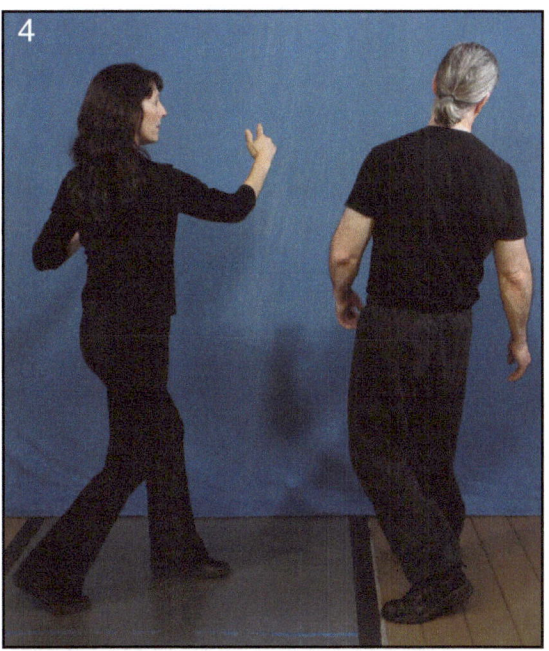

Attacker follows through by twisting the body, the arm drops naturally.

Attacker makes EYE CONTACT to Cue the Backhand Slap.

The slapping hand passes in front of the face at cheekbone level.

Attacker follows through allowing the body to open, and the arm drops naturally.

The recipient twists his body in reaction to the slap.

NOTES: Images 1- 8 show the continous arm action from front hand to back hand slap. These actions can be practiced and performed separately.

Creating the knap, or the sound of the strike, and hiding the air space to make the slap 'read' will be discussed thoroughly in Basics Level 2.

CROSSING PUNCH

A PUNCH is a strike with the fist. A proper fist is made by rolling the fingers closed, and tucking the thumb over the first two fingers.

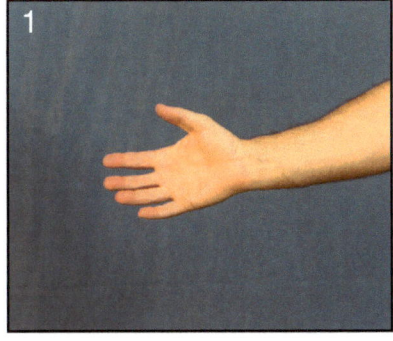

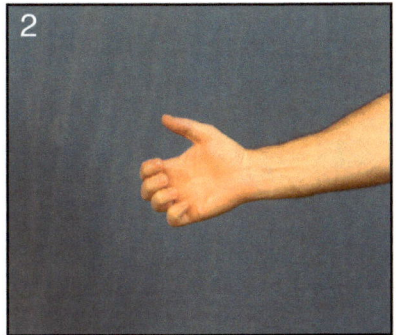

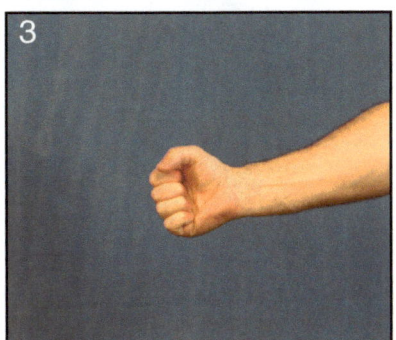

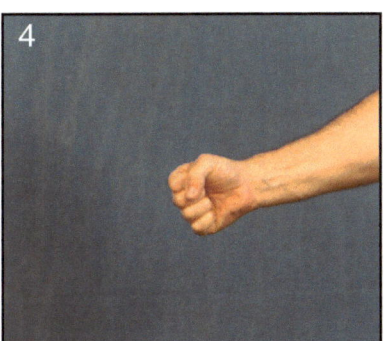

There should be a straight alignment from the forearm, through the wrist to the first two knuckles.

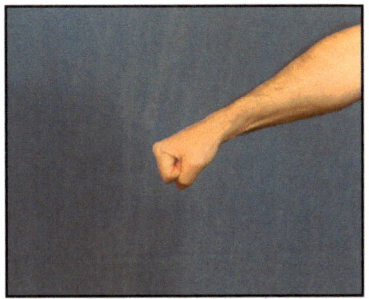

The CROSSING PUNCH gets it name because it crosses the plane of the face from one side to the other, striking the face sideways. Start by SQUARING UP, MEASURING FINGERTIP DISTANCE and finding your FIGHT STANCE.

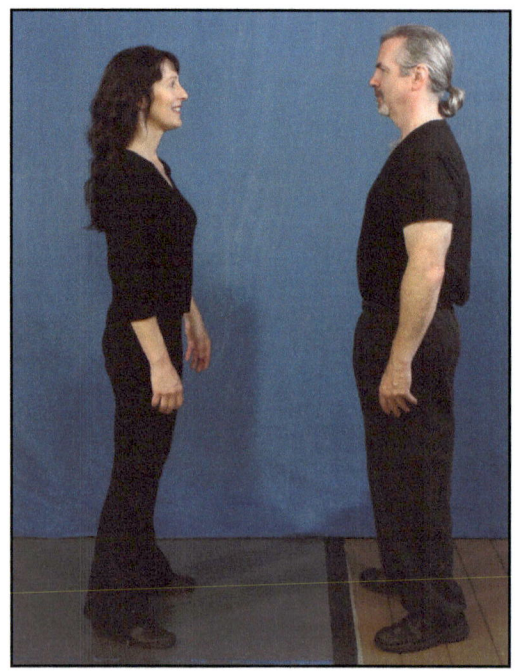

Square up with your partner

Measure fingertip distance

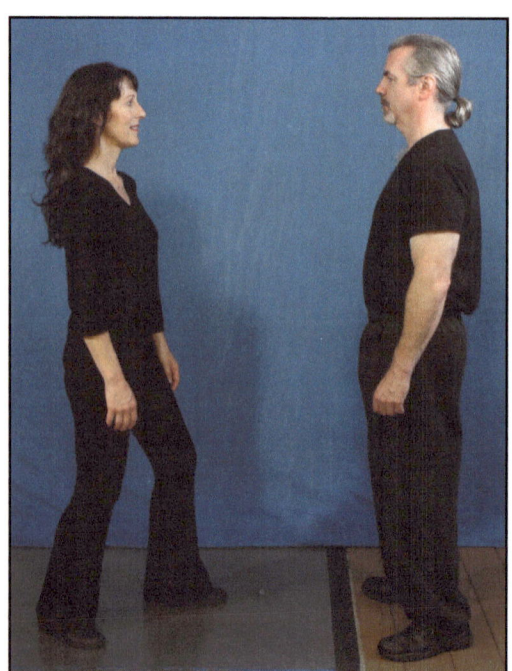

Fight Stance

Then do the THREE PART CUE similar to the slap, except the VISUAL CUE will be a fist with the inside of the hand facing your own cheek. Make sure your arm is relaxed with the elbow down.

NOTE: Keep your punching hand in your peripheral vision.

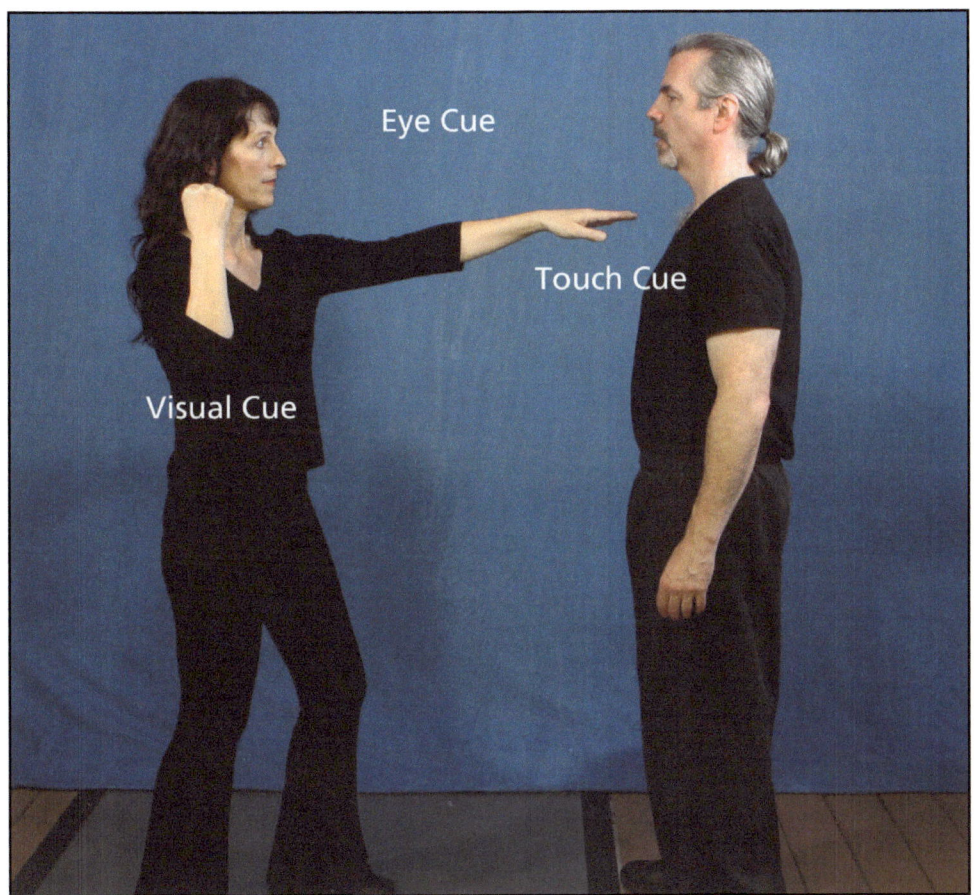

3 Part Cue for the Crossing Punch

Punch by crossing your partner's face at cheekbone level from one side of their face to the other, aiming the first 2-3 knuckles across the target and relaxing the punching arm so it can drop down naturally after "impact." You can create the illusion of impact by using REVERSAL OF TENSION like we do with sword fighting. The TOUCH CUE arm counters the move by recoiling in.

It helps to practice how the energy feels as it is redirected on impact by punching a padded object, such as focus pads for martial arts or boxing training. Be careful how hard you hit, especially at first, so you don't injure yourself.

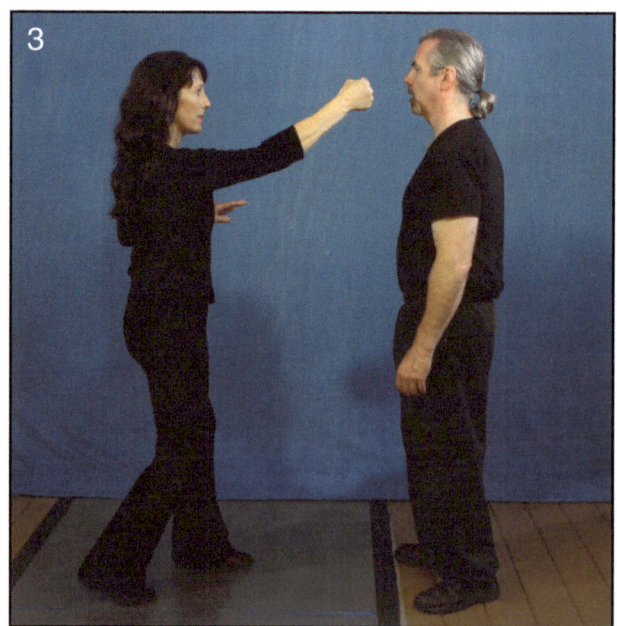

The punching hand passes in front of the face at cheekbone level.

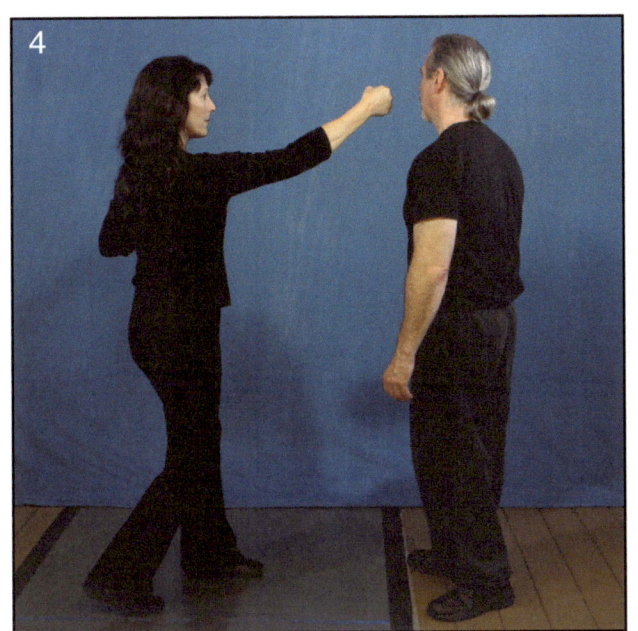

NOTE: Hiding the air space to make the punch 'read' will be discussed thoroughly in Basics Level 2.

QUARTERSTAFF

The QUARTERSTAFF is basically a stick, 5 - 7 feet long. The actual length of each staff is based on the height of the individual using it. They are roughly 1 1/4 inches in diameter. Although traditionally made of oak, a solid hardwood such as hickory or ash can also be used. In early times their ends were commonly shod with iron. The name comes from the way the staff is gripped. It is held BY ITS QUARTERS or in a QUARTERING GRIP.

Parts of the Quarterstaff

A middle and two ends.

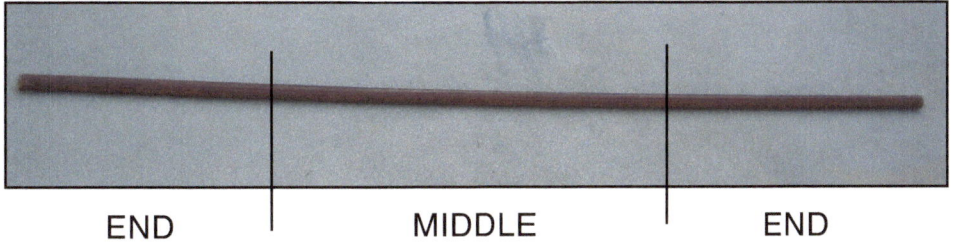

END | MIDDLE | END

Gripping the Quarterstaff

The staff is held in an "over and under" grip with the right hand "under" (palm up).

Footwork

All QUARTERSTAFF FOOTWORK is the same as BROADSWORD FOOTWORK. The quarterstaff technique incorporates a very relaxed spiraling (or twisting) of the body on both ATTACKS and PARRIES.

QUARTERSTAFF PARRY SYSTEM

In the BRITISH QUARTERSTAFF system, parries are given the name of the target (head, chest, shoulder, etc.), but the Academy has assigned numbers to the parries that roughly correspond with the parry numbers of the broadsword. Numbering the quarterstaff parries is helpful to the learning process because you can speak precisely about the move that is required. Keeping the arms bent to provide a muscular cushion and moving the staff into approximations of the broadsword parries gives us the basic Quarterstaff Parry system pictured below.

PARRIES 1 thru Low 5 are made with the MIDDLE of the staff and PARRIES 6 thru 10 are made with the ENDS of the staff.

SAFETY NOTE:

When practicing Quarterstaff Parries, make sure your hands are always clear of the target as you grip the staff. Punching the incoming staff by accident can be very painful...

PARRY 1: The staff is held high at an angle to **protect the Left Shoulder**.

PARRY 2: Hold the staff straight up and down to the right at belly level to **protect the Ribs.**

PARRY 3: The staff is held high at an angle to **protect the Right Shoulder.**

PARRY 4: Hold the staff straight up and down to the left at belly level to **protect the Ribs.**

PARRY 5: The staff is held horizontally out in front of and above the head to **protect the Head.**

The Head can be attacked easily with either the right or left hand leading.

PARRY LOW 5: The staff is held horizontally at mid thigh to **protect the Groin.**

The Groin can be attacked easily with either the right or left hand leading.

PARRY 7: The lower end of the staff is used to **protect the Left Knee.** (Right Hand is down.)

PARRY 8: The lower end of the staff is used to **protect the Right Knee**. (Left Hand is down.)

PARRY 9: The upper end of the staff is used to **protect the Left Cheek**. (Right Hand is up.)

PARRY 10: The upper end of the staff is used to **protect the Right Cheek**. (Left Hand is up.)

Parries 7-10 work very well for BEAT-AWAY, or FLYING PARRIES which deflect the attack by sweeping it away from the target.

DISTANCE and CONTROLLING THE ENERGY of the strike are critical safety factors.

Controlling the Energy of the strike can be accomplished using REVERSAL OF TENSION and stopping the attacks just outside your partner's MAGIC FORCE FIELD.

PARRY 6: The lower end of the staff sweeps up in an arc to **deflect a thrust to the Belly. This parry is not commonly used and is not included in the Basic Quarterstaff Parry Drills.**

Parry 6 prep position.

The end of your staff sweeps your partner's thrust up and to the right.

QUARTERSTAFF DRILLS

Footwork for these drills is mostly Changes of Guard, with Advances and Retreats used as needed to keep the quarterstaff to your open side. It is not incorrect to use the quarterstaff on the opposite side, but most people feel more balanced keeping the staff to the open side.

Quarterstaff Drill 1

A	B
On Guard with Left Foot Forward	On Guard with Left Foot Forward
Right Hand Lead, Change Guard Forward and Attack Left Shoulder	Change Guard Back and Parry 1
Left Hand Lead, Change Guard Forward and Attack Right Ribs	Change Guard Back and Parry 2
Right Hand Lead, Change Guard Forward and Attack Head	Change Guard Back and Parry 5
Left Hand Lead, Change Guard Forward and Attack Groin	Change Guard Back and Parry Low 5
Change Guard Back and Parry 1	Right Hand Lead, Change Guard Forward and Attack Left Shoulder
Change Guard Back and Parry 2	Left Hand Lead, Change Guard Forward and Attack Right Ribs
Change Guard Back and Parry 5	Right Hand Lead, Change Guard Forward and Attack Head
Change Guard Back and Parry Low 5	Left Hand Lead, Change Guard Forward and Attack Groin

Jan instructs Janeshia Adams-Ginyard on the quarterstaff parries.

Quaterstaff Drill 2

A	B
On Guard with Right Foot Forward	On Guard with Right Foot Forward
Left Hand Lead, Change Guard Forward and Attack Right Shoulder	Change Guard Back and Parry 3
Right Hand Lead, Change Guard Forward and Attack Left Ribs	Change Guard Back and Parry 4
Left Hand Lead, Change Guard Forward and Attack Head	Change Guard Back and Parry 5
Right Hand Lead, Change Guard Forward and Attack Groin	Change Guard Back and Parry Low 5
Change Guard Back and Parry 3	Left Hand Lead, Change Guard Forward and Attack Right Shoulder
Change Guard Back and Parry 4	Right Hand Lead, Change Guard Forward and Attack Left Ribs
Change Guard Back and Parry 5	Left Hand Lead, Change Guard Forward and Attack Head
Change Guard Back and Parry Low 5	Right Hand Lead, Change Guard Forward and Attack Groin

Olivia Schlueter-Corey and Josh Rubinstein on set for FIGHT NIGHT, where Academy students perform their fight exams on location for camera.

Quarterstaff Drill 3

A	B
On Guard with Left Foot Forward	On Guard with Left Foot Forward
Right Hand Lead, Change Guard Forward and Attack Left Knee	Change Guard Back Flying Parry 7
Left Hand Lead, Change Guard Forward and Attack Right Knee	Flip the staff so the Left hand is down, Change Guard Back Flying Parry 8
Right Hand Lead, Change Guard Forward and Attack Left Cheek	Change Guard Back, Flying Parry 9
Left Hand Lead, Change Guard Forward and Attack Right Cheek	Change Guard Back, Flip the staff so Left Hand is up, Flying Parry 10
Change Guard Back Flying Parry 7	Right Hand Lead, Change Guard Forward and Attack Left Knee
Flip the staff so the Left hand is down, Change Guard Back Flying Parry 8	Left Hand Lead, Change Guard Forward and Attack Right Knee
Change Guard Back, Flying Parry 9	Right Hand Lead, Change Guard Forward and Attack Left Cheek
Change Guard Back, Flip the staff so Left Hand is up, Flying Parry 10	Left Hand Lead, Change Guard Forward and Attack Right Cheek

Dan and Jan in on guard positions for the Quarterstaff Basic Fight.

Quarterstaff Combined Drill

To combine the Quarterstaff drills, continue from one drill to another without going back to on guard. The transitions from one drill to the next will call for the attacker to advance and the attackee to retreat rather than change guard as in the individual drills. The transitions are in bold print in the choreography grid on the next page.

A	B
On Guard with Left Foot Forward	On Guard with Left Foot Forward
Right Hand Lead, Change Guard Forward and Attack Left Shoulder	Change Guard Back and Parry 1
Left Hand Lead, Change Guard Forward and Attack Right Ribs	Change Guard Back and Parry 2
Right Hand Lead, Change Guard Forward and Attack Head	Change Guard Back and Parry 5
Left Hand Lead, Change Guard Forward and Attack Groin	Change Guard Back and Parry Low 5
Change Guard Back and Parry 1	Right Hand Lead, Change Guard Forward and Attack Left Shoulder
Change Guard Back and Parry 2	Left Hand Lead, Change Guard Forward and Attack Right Ribs
Change Guard Back and Parry 5	Right Hand Lead, Change Guard Forward and Attack Head
Change Guard Back and Parry Low 5	Left Hand Lead, Change Guard Forward and Attack Groin
Left Hand Lead, Advance and Attack Right Shoulder	**Retreat and Parry 3**
Right Hand Lead, Change Guard Forward and Attack Left Ribs	Change Guard Back and Parry 4
Left Hand Lead, Change Guard Forward and Attack Head	Change Guard Back and Parry 5
Right Hand Lead, Change Guard Forward and Attack Groin	Change Guard Back and Parry Low 5
Change Guard Back and Parry 3	Left Hand Lead, Change Guard Forward and Attack Right Shoulder
Change Guard Back and Parry 4	Right Hand Lead, Change Guard Forward and Attack Left Ribs
Change Guard Back and Parry 5	Left Hand Lead, Change Guard Forward and Attack Head
Change Guard Back and Parry Low 5	Right Hand Lead, Change Guard Forward and Attack Groin
Right Hand Lead, Advance and Attack Left Knee	**Retreat Flying Parry 7**
Left Hand Lead, Change Guard Forward and Attack Right Knee	Flip the staff so the Left hand is down, Change Guard Back Flying Parry 8
Right Hand Lead, Change Guard Forward and Attack Left Cheek	Change Guard Back, Flying Parry 9
Left Hand Lead, Change Guard Forward and Attack Right Cheek	Change Guard Back, Flip the staff so Left Hand is up, Flying Parry 10
Change Guard Back Flying Parry 7	Right Hand Lead, Change Guard Forward and Attack Left Knee
Flip the staff so the Left hand is down, Change Guard Back Flying Parry 8	Left Hand Lead, Change Guard Forward and Attack Right Knee
Change Guard Back, Flying Parry 9	Right Hand Lead, Change Guard Forward and Attack Left Cheek
Change Guard Back, Flip the staff so Left Hand is up, Flying Parry 10	Left Hand Lead, Change Guard Forward and Attack Right Cheek

QUARTERSTAFF BASIC FIGHT CHOREOGRAPHY

A	B
On Guard with Left foot Forward, Hands are held low with Right Hand Back	On Guard Right foot Forward with staff pointed at partner Right Hand Forward
Beat B's staff aside with Right End	Accept Beat
Pass Forward and Attack Head with Left	Pass Back Parry 5
Change Guard Forward Attack Ribs with Right	Change Guard Back Parry 4
Change Guard Forward with Lunge and Attack Knee with Left	Change Guard Back Parry 8
Accept Bind	Bind
Jump Back to evade Belly Swipe	(Cue: 1. Lift Staff/ Make Eye Contact, 2. Look to Belly) Swipe Belly with Left
React to Feint	Pass Forward Right Hand Feint to Shoulder
With Right Foot Back Parry 3	Change Guard Forward Attack Shoulder with Left
Change Guard Back and Parry 7	Change Guard Forward Attack Knee with Right
Change Guard Back (spin staff so left hand is down) Parry 8	Change Guard Forward Attack Knee with Left
Change Guard Back Parry 1	Advance Attack Shoulder with Right
Bind to Parry 5	Accept Bind
Change Guard Forward to Place Left Foot on Upper Thigh	Recover balance
Push - Step down on Left foot	'Stumble' Back from push
(Cue: 1. Lift Staff/ Make Eye Contact, 2. Look to Belly) Swipe Belly with Right	Jump Back to evade Belly Swipe
Run Forward Feint to Shoulder with Left	React to Feint
Right Foot Change Guard Forward Attack Knee with Right	Left Foot Change Guard Back Parry 7
Change Guard Back Parry 3	Change Guard Forward Attack Shoulder with Left
Advance Attack Knee with Left	Retreat Parry 8
Change Guard Back Parry 1	Change Guard Forward Attack Shoulder with Right
Lunge Attack Head with Right	Retreat Parry 5
Accept Bind (twisting the body)	Bind Staff to the ground, moving Left to Right, while Changing Guard Forward
React to Punch and Fall to Ground	Crossing punch with Left Hand

To see performance videos of the Quarterstaff Basic Fight, visit us on
Youtube.com/AcademyFightClass

Coming Soon:

Academy of Theatrical Combat

Basics Level II

Double Cutlass
Advanced Cutlass
Advanced Broadsword

About the Sword Masters

Dan Speaker

Dan Speaker (*Master and Commander, Hidalgo, Hot Shots Part Deux*, and more) has been fascinated with swords and weaponry all his life. Since early childhood, he studied martial arts, fencing, horseback riding, and even learned to play the Highland Bagpipe. In his teens he became involved with theatre, and began to study how to use combat in performance. This culminated in studying at the Royal Scottish Academy of Music and Drama where he obtained a Diploma in Dramatic Arts and a Fencing Coach's credential.

Working in theatre as an actor and fight choreographer, he met his wife-to-be, dance choreographer turned swordswoman, Jan Bryant. Together they moved to Hollywood and created a new method of teaching and choreographing the art of combat for film. Their career has spanned from putting together Bruce Campbell's iconic action on *Army of Darkness* to training Russell Crowe and choreographing all the fights on *Master and Commander.*

Go to Theatricalcombat.com for Dan's complete professional resume or contact him by e-mail at dan@theatricalcombat.com.

Jan Bryant

Jan Bryant (*Master and Commander, Hook, Army of Darkness,* and more) was a dancer and choreographer of dance, and a horseback-riding enthusiast who had always been interested in the art of combat. Her interest in sword fighting was kindled by romantic historical pieces glorified by early movie swashbucklers. Unable to find sword fighting as an art form she could train in as a child she took dance classes instead. Eventually attending and graduating from UC Berkeley with a degree in theatre, Jan focused on telling stories through movement. The real shift in her career came when she was working in regional theater and met her husband-to-be, Dan Speaker. They moved to Hollywood and melded their respective talents and training into a new method of teaching and choreographing fight scenes for the motion picture industry.

Today Jan is one of the only female sword masters in the entire film industry, and continues to teach, choreograph and perform the arts of combat and sword fighting. She uses her talents in all aspects of cinematic fight design and action, from training Robin Williams and Dustin Hoffman when she and Dan were the sword masters on *Hook* to wielding a blade herself as Catherine Zeta-Jones's sword fighting double in *The Mask of Zorro.* Occasionally she even gets to race through the woods on horseback in romantic action films!

Go to Theatricalcombat.com for Jan's complete professional resume or contact her by e-mail at jan@theatricalcombat.com.

Dan and Jan are now considered to be among the top sword fighting choreographers in film today, and as a sword fighting/action team, their work is unparalleled the world over.

Kim Turney

Kim Turney considers herself to be a 21st century artist. Graduating with two degrees in acting from Ohio State University, she continued to pursue many interests in the entertainment world. She worked in film marketing with Disney's Buena Vista Pictures and Distribution, stunt doubled, stunt coordinated and assistant sword mastered on many different film projects such as *The Lady Musketeer* (Hallmark)*, A Dead Calling,* and *The Grim Reaper*.

Kim studied digital cameras extensively and worked on the first fully digital workflow film project in Los Angeles in 2006. She created and taught digital filmmaking and video game design classes to children grades K - 12 with Freshi Films, LLC, and produced the web series *Perils of the Pirate Princess*. Along with Dan and Jan, she recently became a Fight Design Choreographer for a new video game with Leviathan Interactive. Currently she writes, produces and directs the Academy of Theatrical Combat's web series *FIGHT CLASS The Series*.

Throughout all of these adventures Kim has been a part of the Academy of Theatrical Combat, reaching the level of Sword Master in 2005 for over 9 years of teaching and training in theatrical combat that culminated in creating and notating all of the fights for the short film *Intervention*. When not swinging swords at the Academy, Kim has a great time updating and maintaining TheatricalCombat.com and utilizing social media to communicate with sword fighters all over the world!

You can contact Kim by e-mail at kim@theatricalcombat.com.

Have fun and thanks for joining us on our
quest to create a better world of theatrical fights for everyone!

Jan, Dan and Kim

Academy of Theatrical Combat Basics Level 1

Sample Theatrical Combat Course Curriculum

15 weeks, 2 classes a week for 2 hours

The goal of the Academy of Theatrical Combat is to give our students/performers all the tools they need to feel confident in any action situation for stage, film, television, motion capture, or internet production. This includes knowing theatrical combat techniques so well, they become second nature and allow the actor to adapt safely to any and all situations they might face as a performer.

Theatrical Combat Course Objectives

Students develop the skills required to perform fight choreography safely and with confidence.

Students perform frequently for the class and for the camera. This will help them learn how to handle performance adrenaline so they can perform their fights safely, accurately, and effectively.

Students develop the ability to adapt to performance situations they might find themselves in during their professional career.

Students' work is filmed so the footage can be used as a training tool. Students should bring their own recording device (a cell phone camera or other) so they can review their own progress and practice between classes.

Students change fight partners frequently so they can adapt to partnering with different body and movement types.

Students fight with the cutlass with both right and left hands to improve learning and coordination as well as balance muscle development.

Note to the Instructor:
The focus of the following curriculum is on learning and performing theatrical combat technique. Assignments requiring scholarly research, presentations, or essays, are left up to your discretion. Feel free to adapt this curriculum to the time frame and facilities available to you.

Week 1

Day 1 Introduce the idea of Theatrical Combat as a movement discipline. Why is it important for actors to learn these skills?

Review Syllabus and Class Objectives

INTRODUCE THE CUTLASS
    Brief history and parts of the cutlass *(p. 7)*.

The Grip - How to hold the cutlass *(p. 8)*.

Introduce the concepts of **Reversal of Tension** and **The Magic Force Field** *(p. 11)*.

FOOTWORK *(p. 9)*
    On Guard
    Advance
    Retreat
    Change Guard Forward
    Change Guard Back
    Pass Forward
    Pass Back
    Demi Lunge

Day 2 Begin class with Footwork Drill. Drill on both the right and left.

    DISTANCE *(p. 10)*
        Out of Distance
        On Guard Distance
        Attack Distance

Cutting - Using the edge both in impact as well as draw cuts *(p. 11)*.

Discuss **Targeting** - Looking at the target. Stopping the blade action at the Force Field *(p. 13)*.

Discuss **Communication With Your Partner** *(p. 13)*.

Cutting Drill - Emphasize relaxation and breathing while doing the drill *(p. 12)*.

Magic Force Field Drill - Emphasize relaxation & breathing while doing the drill *(p. 12)*.

Introduce **Attacks** - Belly, Flank, Shoulder, Chest, Head, Groin, Head *(pp. 14-17)*
Introduce **Parries** - 1, 2, 3, 4, 5, 7, 9 *(pp. 18-26)*

Week 2

Day 3 Begin class with Footwork Drill. Drill on both the right and left.

Review Cutting to Target - Belly, Flank, Shoulder, Chest, Head, Groin, Head

Review Parries - 1, 2, 3, 4, 5, 7, 9

Practice cutting with advances.
Practice parries with retreats.

Basic Cutlass Drill #1 - Learn drill with both right and left hand *(p. 27)*.
Rotate partners throughout class.

Day 4 Begin class with **Basic Hand to Hand**.

HAND TO HAND *(pp. 49-61)*
   Twisting Drill

   Setting up Distance and Cueing

   Slaps: Forehand, Backhand, and Reactions

   Crossing Punch and Reaction

Basic Cutlass Drill #1- Drill with right and left hand.

Introduce Basic Cutlass Drill #2- Learn drill with both right and left hand *(p. 28)*.

Week 3

Day 5 Begin class with Footwork Drill. Drill on both the right and left.

Practice cutting with advances.
Practice parries with retreats.

Basic Cutlass Drill #1 - Drill with right and left hand.
Basic Cutlass Drill #2 - Drill with right and left hand.

Perform Basic Cutlass Drills #1 and #2 for the class, classmates can record the fights so performers have a copy on their own cameras.

INTRODUCE BROADSWORD
   Brief History including why we do right hand lead only *(p. 33)*.
   Broadsword **On Guard**, Broadsword **Footwork**, **Cutting** with the Broadsword *(pp. 34-35)*

   Introduce the concept of **Wringing Contraction** *(p. 35)*.

Day 6 Begin class with Basic Hand to Hand.

Slaps: Forehand, Backhand, and Reactions
Crossing Punches and Reactions

Broadsword Attacks - Belly, Flank, Shoulder, Chest, Head, Groin, Head

Broadsword Parries - 1, 2, 3, 4, 5, 7, 9 *(p. 36-44)*

Broadsword Drill #1 *(p. 47)*
Broadsword Drill #2 - with mixed footwork *(p. 47)*

Basic Cutlass Drill #1- Drill with right and left hand.
Basic Cutlass Drill #2- Drill with right and left hand.

Week 4

Day 7 Begin class with Footwork Drill. Drill on both the right and left.

Basic Cutlass Drill #1- Drill with right and left hand.
Basic Cutlass Drill #2- Drill with right and left hand.

Introduce Bind Swipe Drill with Cutlass *(p. 29)*.

Introduce Quarterstaff -
    Brief History - Etymology and gripping the quarterstaff *(p. 63)*.

Quarterstaff **Parries** - 1, 2, 3, 4, 5, low 5, 7, 8, 9, 10 *(pp. 64-75)*
Quarterstaff **Attacks** - Left Shoulder, Right Ribs, Right Shoulder, Left Ribs, Head,
    Groin, Left Knee, Right Knee, Left check Right Cheek

Quarterstaff Drill #1 *(p. 76)*
Quarterstaff Drill #2 *(p. 77)*
Quarterstaff Drill #3 *(p. 78)*

Day 8 Begin class with Basic Hand to Hand.

Slaps: Forehand, Backhand, and Reactions, Crossing Punch.

Broadsword Drill #1
Broadsword Drill #2 - with mixed footwork.
Perform Broadsword Drills for class and their own cameras.

Quarterstaff Drill #1, #2 and #3

Basic Cutlass Drill #1 - Drill with right and left hand.
Basic Cutlass Drill #2- Drill with right and left hand.

Week 5

Day 9 Begin class with Footwork Drill. Drill on both the right and left.

Broadsword Drill #1
Broadsword Drill #2 - with mixed footwork.

Basic Cutlass Drill #1- Drill with right and left hand.
Basic Cutlass Drill #2- Drill with right and left hand.

Bind Swipe Drill with Cutlass

Begin working on **Cutlass Basic Fight Choreography** *(p. 31)*.
    Students must learn both sides of the fight with right and left hands.
    Focus on partnering and partnered techniques,
    Being in the moment, reacting to what is in front of them and
    Phrasing the fight.

End class with performing at least a portion of the fight.

Day 10 Begin class with **Quarterstaff Drill #1, #2 and #3**

Perform Quarterstaff Drills for the class and their own cameras.

Continue working on **Cutlass Basic Fight Choreography**
    Students must learn both sides of the fight with right and left hands.
    Perform part of fight for class and their own cameras.

Week 6

Day 11 Begin class with Footwork Drill. Drill on both the right and left.

Broadsword Drill #1
Broadsword Drill #2 - mixed footwork

Bind Swipe Drill with Broadsword *(p. 46)*.

Begin working on **Broadsword Basic Fight Choreography** *(p. 48)*.
    Students must learn both sides of the fight.
    Focus on partnering and partnered techniques.
    Being in the moment.
    Phrasing the fight.

Basic Cutlass Drill #1- Drill with right and left hand.
Basic Cutlass Drill #2- Drill with right and left hand.

Basic Cutlass Fight - Work with different partners for both right and left hand.

Day 12 Begin class with Basic Hand to Hand.

>Continue working on **Broadsword Basic Fight Choreography.**
>>Students must learn both sides of the fight.
>
>**Quarterstaff Drill Combined Version** *(p. 78)*

Perform One Side of the **Basic Cutlass Fight** for class and their own cameras.

Week 7

Day 13 Begin class with Footwork Drill. Drill on both the right and left.

>**BASIC CUTLASS FIGHT TEST**
>>Students warm up the **Cutlass Basic Fight** with their performance partners.
>>Students perform the **Cutlass Basic Fight** - Sides A & B on right and left.
>
>Students perform each side of the fight 3 times.
>>First performance for Proscenium Audience
>>Second Performance for Camera Angle 1
>>Third Performance for Camera Angle 2
>
>Students review test fight footage with the instructor during office hours.

Day 14 Finish up filming **Cutlass Basic Fights** for review.
>Students warm up the **Cutlass Basic Fight** with their performance partners.
>Students perform the **Cutlass Basic Fight** - Sides A & B on right and left.
>
>Students review fight footage with the instructor during office hours.
>
>**Broadsword Drill #1**
>**Broadsword Drill #2 -** with mixed footwork.
>
>Continue working on **Broadsword Basic Fight Choreography.**
>>Students must learn both sides of the fight.
>>Perform all or part of the broadsword fight for their own cameras.
>
>**Quarterstaff Drill Combined Version**

Week 8

Day 15 Begin class with **Basic Cutlass Fight** - as a warm up.

Quarterstaff Drills Combined Version
Perform Quarterstaff drills for the class and their own cameras.

Broadsword Basic Fight - Prep for performance
End class with **Broadsword Basic Fight** - One side only. May be filmed with their own cameras.

Day 16 Begin class with **Basic Broadsword Fight** - as a warm up.

BASIC BROADSWORD FIGHT TEST

Students Perform the **Broadsword Basic Fight** - Sides A & B

Students perform each side of the fight 3 times.
 First performance for Proscenium Audience
 Second Performance for Camera Angle 1
 Third Performance for Camera Angle 2

Students review fight footage with the instructor during office hours.

Week 9

Day 17 Begin class with **Basic Broadsword Fight** - as a warm up.

Finish BASIC BROADSWORD FIGHT TEST

Quarterstaff Drills Combined Version

Begin working on **Quarterstaff Basic Fight Choreography** *(p. 80)*.
 Students must learn both sides of the fight.

Day 18 Begin class with Basic Hand to Hand.

Quarterstaff Drills Combined Version

Continue working on **Quarterstaff Basic Fight Choreography**
 Students must learn both sides of the fight.

End class with **Quarterstaff Basic Fight performance** - either part of or whole fight (one side only) for class and their own cameras.

Week 10

Day 19 Begin class with **Cutlass Drills #1 & #2**.

    Cutlass Basic Fight as a warm up.

    Quarterstaff Drills Combined Version

    Continue working on **Quarterstaff Basic Fight Choreography**
        Students must learn both sides of the fight.

    End class with **Cutlass Basic Fight** review.

Day 20 Begin class with Basic Hand to hand.

    Broadsword Drills #1 & #2

    Broadsword Basic Fight as a warm up.

    Quarterstaff Drills Combined Version

    Continue working on **Quarterstaff Basic Fight Choreography.**
        Students must learn both sides of the fight.
        Prep **Quarterstaff Basic Fight** for performance.

    End class with **Quarterstaff Basic Fight**. Perform one side of fight for the class and their own cameras.

Week 11

Day 21 QUARTERSTAFF BASIC FIGHT TEST

    Students Perform the **Quarterstaff Basic Fight** - Sides A & B.

    Students perform each side of the fight 3 times.
        First performance for Proscenium Audience
        Second Performance for Camera Angle 1
        Third Performance for Camera Angle 2

    Students review fight footage with the instructor during office hours.

Day 22 Begin class with **Quarterstaff Drills Combined Version**

    Finish **Quarterstaff Basic Fight Test.**

    Students review fight footage with the instructor during office hours.

Week 12

Day 23 Warm up with **Cutlass Drills #1 & #2 and Basic Cutlass Fight.**

    ALTERNATE TERRAIN ASSIGNMENT

        Depending on the weather - Students find alternative settings to perform the **Cutlass, Broadsword, or Quarterstaff Basic Fight** - on gravel, grass, stairs, etc.
        All students adapt their fight to the new terrain, making adjustments in movement and distance as needed.
        Fight pairs perform their fights in their separate locations for the rest of the class. May be performed for their own cameras.

        After each performance, discuss as a class the challenges that were created by the different terrain. How did the students deal with them?

Day 24 Warm up with **Cutlass Drills #1 & #2 and Basic Cutlass Fight.**

    Complete the **ALTERNATE TERRAIN ASSIGNMENT**

Week 13

Day 25 Technique Review
    Cutlass Drills #1 & #2, Cutlass Basic Fight

    With new partner, **Broadsword Drills #1 & #2, Broadsword Basic Fight**

    With a third partner, **Quarterstaff Drills Combined Version, Quarterstaff Basic Fight**

    Perform the drills and fights for the class and their own cameras.

Day 26 Class works together to create a **Melee Performance**.

    Students choose weapons and beginning partners.
    Students use choreography elements they have learned performing the basic fights to create short sequences.
    The melee continues until there is only one fighter left.

    For example: Beginning Partners are A-B, C-D, E-F, G-H, J-K, L-M.
    Winners of the first round fight each other A-D, E-H, J-M.
    The last fight could be A against H and M - with M being the last Performer standing.

    As a class, decide on the story of the fight.
        Who are these people? Why are they here? Why are they fighting?

    NOTE: There is to be no dialogue, the story must be told through the actions of the performers.

Week 14

Day 27 Begin class with Footwork Drill.

Melee Rehearsal

Focus on the staging of the fights, how one fight flows into another.

Focus on the performer's awareness of everyone around them. They are each responsible for their partners safety throughout the melee.

Performers must take into consideration that there will be dead bodies to fight around in the later fights of the melee.

Day 28 Technique Review

Cutlass Drills #1 & #2

Broadsword Drills #1 & #2

Quarterstaff Drills Combined Version

Perform each portion of the Melee Fight for the class. Use their own cameras to assess what they need to work on outside of class.

Week 15

Day 29 Melee Rehearsal in performance space.

The performance space can be a stage, soundstage, or alternate terrain.

Day 30 Final Class Performance of the Melee Fight.

First performance for Proscenium Audience
Second Performance for Camera Angle 1
Third Performance for Camera Angle 2

Appendix

The following assessment grids are suggestions from the Sword Masters based on the ongoing training classes at the Academy of Theatrical Combat in Burbank, California.

> Generic Assessment Grid for all Weapons *(below)*
>
> Annotated Assessment Grids for *Academy of Theatrical Combat Basics Level 1*
>
> > Cutlass *(p. 99)*
> >
> > Broadsword *(p. 101)*
> >
> > Quarterstaff *(p. 103)*

Generic Assessment Grid for All Weapons

	A	B	C	D	E
Footwork	Foot Alignment	Body Alignment	Steps and Timing	Front Foot Heel	Back Foot Edge
Distance and Targeting	On Guard Distance	First Attack Distance	Maintain Correct Distance	Looking to Target	Cutting Accurately to Target
Parry Positions	Arm Alignment	Blade Alignment	Edge Alignment	Parry Placement	
Grip and Cutting Action	Fingers Relaxed	Proper Grip	Cutting Action	Weapon Control Throughout Drill	
Relaxation and Breathing	Shoulders Relaxed and Down	Grip Firm and Relaxed	Face Relaxed and Supple and Eyes have Roving Focus	Breathing Throughout the Drill	In the Moment with Their Partner, Reacting to What is Happening

Annotated Performance Assessment for Cutlass

	A	B	C	D	E
Footwork	Foot Alignment: Are the front foot and knee pointing straight forward while back foot/knee are pointing to outside at 90 degrees?	Body Alignment: Are they facing 3/4 front and lined up with their partner's center? Is their weight distributed 50/50 on their feet?	Steps and Timing: Are they clearing the ground but not lifting the feet too high? Is the cadence of footwork matching the heartbeat and working in time with cuts and parries?	Is the Front Foot reaching with the heel on forward movements, pushing off the heel to move backwards?	Is the Back Foot pushing off the entire back edge of the foot on forward movements and reaching with the back edge to move backwards?
Distance and Targeting	Do they have a good on guard distance?	Can they compress the distance accurately on their first attack?	Are they able to maintain correct distance for each attack?	Are the cuts coming in accurately towards the targets on their partner's body?	Are they looking to target on their partner's body and stopping the cut at the "magic force field?"
Parry Positions	Arm Alignment: Is the arm and wrist alignment correct on all parry positions creating optimal skeletal alignment for strength?	Blade Alignment: Is the Forte section of the blade in front of the target?	Edge alignment: Does the edge meet the incoming blade's edge?	Parry Placement: Are the parries out in front of the body - creating the "force field?"	
Grip and Cutting Action	Are their fingers relaxed and wrapped holding the handle into the palm of the hand (*hypothenar eminence*)?	Are they maintaining proper grip both on attacks and parries?	Do they flex their wrist, keeping the point of the weapon in their peripheral vision, in preparation for the cut?	Are they maintaining control of the blade after each cut? Hitting too hard or not hard enough?	Does the impact cut look like a real chop at the targets?
Relaxation and Breathing	Are their shoulders relaxed and down throughout the drill?	Is the grip on the cutlass firm and relaxed?	Is their face relaxed and supple? Are their eyes free to look anywhere necessary?	Are they breathing throughout the drill?	Are they in the moment with their partner, reacting to what is happening?

Annotated Performance Assessment for Broadsword

	A	B	C	D	E
Footwork	Foot Alignment: Is the Front foot/knee pointing straight forward while back foot/knee are pointing to outside at 90 degrees, with the back foot able to pivot as needed?	Body Alignment: Are they lined up with their partner's center? Is their weight distributed 50/50 on their feet?	Steps and Timing: Are they clearing the ground but not lifting the feet too high? Is the cadence of footwork matching the heartbeat, and working in time with cuts and parries?	Is the Front Foot reaching with the heel on forward movements, pushing off the heel to move backwards?	Are they pushing off the entire back edge or ball of the Back Foot on forward movements and reaching with the back edge or ball of the Back Foot to move backwards?
Distance and Targeting	Do they have a good on guard distance?	Can they compress the distance accurately on their first attack?	Are they able to maintain correct distance for each attack?	Are the cuts coming in accurately towards the targets on their partner's body?	Are they looking to target on their partner's body and stopping the cut at the "magic force field?"
Parry Positions	Arm Alignment: Is the arm and wrist alignment correct on all parry positions creating optimal skeletal alignment for strength?	Blade Alignment: Is the Forte section of the blade in front of the target?	Edge alignment: Does the edge meet the incoming blade's edge?	Parry Placement: Are the parries out in front of the body - creating the "force field?"	
Grip and Cutting Action	Are their fingers relaxed and wrapped? Is the Front hand grip firm, back hand mobile and relaxed on the pommel?	Are they maintaining proper grip both on attacks and parries.	Do they flex their wrist, keeping the point of the weapon in their peripheral vision, in preparation for the cut?	Are they maintaining control of the blade after each cut? Hitting too hard or not hard enough? Using Wringing Contraction for control?	Does the impact cut look like a real chop at the targets? Are they using the rotation of the body to make the attacks look powerful?
Relaxation and Breathing	Are their shoulders relaxed and down throughout the drill?	Is the grip on the broadsword firm and relaxed?	Is their face relaxed and supple? Are their eyes free to look anywhere necessary?	Are they breathing throughout the drill?	Are they in the moment with their partner, reacting to what is happening?

Annotated Performance Assessment for Quarterstaff

	A	B	C	D	E
Footwork	Foot Alignment: Is the front foot and knee pointing straight forward while back foot/knee are pointing to outside? Is the back foot placement fluid to accommodate optimal weapon use?	Body Alignment: Are they lined up with their partner's centers? Is their weight distributed 50/50 on their feet?	Steps and Timing: Are they clearing the ground but not lifting the feet too high? Is their footwork working in time with their parries and attacks?	Is the Front Foot reaching with the heel on forward movements, pushing off the heel to move backwards?	Are they pushing off the entire back edge or ball of the Back Foot on forward movements and reaching with the back edge or ball of the foot to move backwards?
Distance and Targeting	Do they have a good on guard distance?	Can they compress the distance accurately on their first attack?	Are they able to maintain correct distance for each attack?	Are the attacks coming in accurately towards the targets on their partner's body?	Are they looking to target on their partner's body and stopping the attack at the "magic force field?"
Parry Positions	Arm Alignment: Are the arm and wrist alignments correct on all parry positions creating optimal skeletal alignment for strength?	Staff Alignment: Do they parry correctly with the center or ends of the staff?	Parry Placement: Are the parries out in front of the body - creating the "force field?"		
Grip and Cutting Action	Are their fingers relaxed and gripping the staff just wider than the shoulders? Are they holding the staff by it's quarters?	Are they maintaining proper grip both on attacks and parries?	Do they keep the ends of the weapon in their peripheral vision, in preparation for the attack?	Are they maintaining control of the staff after each cut? Hitting too hard or not hard enough?	Does the impact attack look like a real chop at the targets? Are they using the rotation of the body to make the attacks look powerful?
Relaxation and Breathing	Are their shoulders relaxed and down throughout the drill?	Is the grip on the staff should be firm and relaxed?	Is their face relaxed and supple? Are their eyes free to look anywhere necessary.?	Are they breathing throughout the drill?	Are they in the moment with their partner, reacting to what is happening?

www.ingramcontent.com/pod-product-compliance
Lightning Source LLC
Chambersburg PA
CBHW041528220426
43671CB00002B/25